Core Geography

The Physical World

Fred Martin and Aubrey Whittle

Hutchinson
London Melbourne Sydney Auckland Johannesburg

Hutchinson Education

An imprint of Century Hutchinson Ltd.
62-65 Chandos Place, London WC2N 4NW

Century Hutchinson Australia Pty Ltd., PO Box 496,
16-22 Church Street, Hawthorn, Victoria 3122, Australia

Century Hutchinson New Zealand Ltd.
PO Box 40-086, Glenfield, Auckland 10, New Zealand

Century Hutchinson South Africa (Pty) Ltd.
PO Box 337, Bergvlei, 2012 South Africa

First published 1987
© Fred Martin and Aubrey Whittle 1987
Typeset in Palatino and Helvetica

Printed and bound by Scotprint

British Library Cataloguing in Publication Data
Martin, Fred
 The physical world — (Core geography)
 1. Physical geography — Text-books —1945-
 I. Title II. Whittle, Aubrey III. Series 910'.02   GB55

ISBN 0 09 164201 9

Acknowledgements

The following are acknowledged for help with information and photographs:

Aerocamera (Bart Hofmeester) pp.69, 122;
Aerofilms Ltd pp.36, 51, 77, 88, 90, 92, 120;
Airviews (Manchester) Ltd p.116;
J Allister pp.48, 49, 50, 63, 67;
Michael Andrews p.42;
Australian Information Service p.99;
L Bahaire pp.38, 61;
Barnaby's Picture Library pp.75, 89;
British Antarctic Survey p.24;
British Geological Survey pp.9, 12, 18, 113;
J Allan Cash pp.7, 28, 30, 32, 117, 123;
Bruce Coleman pp.49, 76, 86, 93, 94, 96;
Colorific p.111;
A Eavis pp.114, 115;
Elf Aquitaine p.21;
FAO pp.44, 45, 56, 57;
Format Photographers (B Prince) p.72;
Geological Society p.39;
Don Green p.121;
Harlow Development Corporation p.55;
John Hildare p.108;
The Hutchison Library p.37;
Michael Jay pp.79, 92;
KLM aerocarto p.122;
N Lancaster pp.95, 106, 107;
Landform Slides pp.28, 31, 34, 50, 77, 78, 94, 98, 104, 116, 118;
Frank Lane Agency pp.29, 82, 87;
Leicestershire County Council: Museums, Art Galleries and Records Service p.27;
M Lowman pp.70, 71;
National Geographic Society p.23;
National Research Council, Canada pp.83, 84, 85;
Network Photographers p.42;
New Zealand Government Tourist Dept. p.25;
Panos Institute pp.42, 43, 44;
Picturepoint Ltd pp.9, 50, 73, 74, 91, 93, 95, 97, 99, 118, 121, 123;
N Roberts p.14;
Royal Geographical Society pp.81 (E Derbyshire), 104, 105;
Science Photo Library pp.11, 97;
A Slater pp.5, 112;
Solarfilma p.110;
Frank Spooner (D Shireff) p.108;
State of Bahrain Water Supply p.101;
M Stone pp.8, 27, 29, 31;
USDA pp.40, 41;
US Geological Survey pp.22, 74;
University of Cambridge, Committee for Aerial Photography pp.87, 89, 119;
Westair p.66;
Western Australian Dept. of Agriculture p.103;
J Wooldridge p.114;
Yorkshire Water Authority p.59.

Contents

UNIT 1
The unstable crust

1.1	Introduction	5
1.2	The Earth machine	6
1.3	Moving plates	10
1.4	Structures and landforms	14
1.5	Geology in action	20

UNIT 2
Breaking the surface

2.1	Introduction	27
2.2	Weather at work	28
2.3	The sloping land	34
2.4	The wasting land	40

UNIT 3
Rivers and coasts

3.1	Introduction	45
3.2	Rivers at work	46
3.3	Rivers; the human impact	54
3.4	The changing coast	60
3.5	Planning the coast	68

UNIT 4
The big freeze

4.1	Introduction	73
4.2	Ice on the move	74
4.3	Danger from ice	80
4.4	Frozen hard	82
4.5	After the ice	86

UNIT 5
The desert scene

5.1	Introduction	93
5.2	Breaking the desert rocks	94
5.3	Desert water	96
5.4	Water for people	100
5.5	Sands of time	104

UNIT 6
Landscapes in change

6.1	Introduction	109
6.2	Volcanic landscapes	110
6.3	A world of peaks and caverns	114
6.4	Chalk landscapes	118
6.5	Landscapes of technology	120

Glossary — 124

Other titles in the Core Geography series

Leisure

1. Leisure in the landscape
2. Leisure in cities
3. Into the countryside
4. Problems and plans
5. Holiday environments
6. Tourism: problems and potential

Work

1. The world of work
2. Work on the land
3. People and industry
4. Change
5. Work and environment

Cities

1. Where people live
2. City systems
3. The unequal city
4. The changing city
5. People in the countryside

The Developing World

1. The poor countries
2. Brakes on progress
3. Worlds of change
4. Signs of strain
5. Choice and conflict

The United Kingdom

1. The land
2. The weather
3. National patterns
4. The South East
5. London
6. The South West
7. The Midlands
8. East Anglia
9. Wales
10. The North West
11. Yorkshire and Humberside
12. The North
13. Scotland
14. Northern Ireland

UNIT 1   The unstable crust

1.1   Introduction

Ancient people worshipped things they did not understand. Gods were blamed when volcanoes erupted, rivers flooded and waves pounded the coast. These were mighty forces to be feared and worshipped (Figure 1).

Physical geography

Today we understand better how natural forces work. Landscapes are carefully measured and described. The forces which shape the land are studied so that events in the future can be predicted. The study of shapes in the landscape is called **geomorphology**.

Figure 1   *The Gods are to blame*

The need to know

Information about geomorphology is needed by people in many types of job (Figure 2). **Geologists** study rocks to find new resources. Civil engineers who build roads, bridges and dams need information about the ground they build on. An understanding of rivers is needed to plan water supplies, navigation, pollution- and flood-control.

For some people, scenery is something to be enjoyed (Figure 3). A better understanding adds to the enjoyment.

Figure 2   *Questions about the landscape*

Figure 3   *Reaching the top of Snowdon*

Exercises

1. a What is studied in geomorphology?
   b Use Figure 2 to give some examples of problems which can be solved with an understanding of geomorphology. For each, such as a farmer or stone mason, say what kind of work would be involved.

2. a How can people 'enjoy' a mountain such as Snowdon?
   b Make a list of some other well-known natural features you know. For each, say what kind of feature it is and where it is.

1.2 The Earth machine

We live on an active planet. The inside is hot and moving. On the surface wind and rain, seas and rivers, growing plants and animals, give our varied and ever changing landscapes.

Inside the earth

Earth was formed about 4500 million years ago. It is one of nine **planets** that orbit the sun to make up the **solar system**.

Earth is made of dense rock that is rich in iron and silicates (Figure 1). The inside is molten hot but there is a cooled outer **crust**. This layer is called the **lithosphere**.

Earth materials by weight

Oxygen 53%
Silicon 26%
Aluminium 7.5%
Iron 4.0%
Calcium 3.5%
Potassium 3.0%
Other 3.0%

SURFACE

CRUST Cooled granite and basalt

MANTLE Iron and magnesium at 1000°C

OUTER CORE Liquid iron and nickel at 3000°C

INNER CORE Solid iron and nickel at 5000°C

70 km
2900 km
5150 km
6371 km

Figure 1 *Inside the Earth*

Water almost everywhere

Oceans and seas make up the Earth's **hydrosphere** (Figure 2). These cover two-thirds of the Earth's surface. The deepest depths are around 11 000 m.

Large land areas called **continents** make up the remaining third. Some places lie below sea level while others reach over 8000 m.

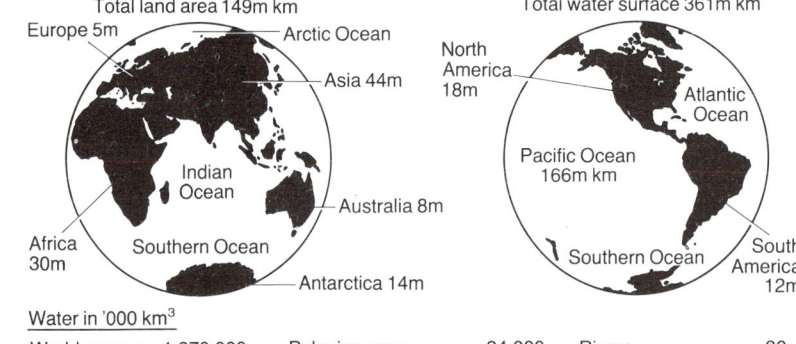

Total land area 149m km
Europe 5m
Arctic Ocean
Asia 44m
Indian Ocean
Australia 8m
Africa 30m
Southern Ocean
Antarctica 14m

Total water surface 361m km
North America 18m
Atlantic Ocean
Pacific Ocean 166m km
Southern Ocean
South America 12m

Water in '000 km³

| World oceans | 1 370 000 | Polar ice caps | 24 000 | Rivers | 80 |
| Groundwater | 60 000 | Surface water on land | 280 | Atmospheric vapour | 14 |

Figure 2 *Continents and oceans*

Exercises

1 Make a copy of Figure 1.

2 a What do you notice about the thickness of the crust compared to the other layers?
   b How do you think the crust was formed?
   c What word is used to describe the central part of the earth?
   d What word describes rock that is so hot, it has melted?
   e Why is rock in the mantle able to flow?

3 a Explain the word 'lithosphere'.
   b Draw a bar graph to show what materials the Earth is made of.

4 On a world outline map, mark in:
   the seven continents
   the five oceans

5 Draw a bar graph to show the sizes of the continents. Arrange the bars in size order with the largest first.

6 a Explain the word 'hydrosphere'.
   b Where are the main areas of ice?
   c How is water moved about in the oceans?
   d Use an atlas to name some of the world's ocean currents. Write down which are hot and which are cold.

A layer of gas

A layer of gases about 8 km deep surrounds the Earth to form the **atmosphere** (Figure 3). Land temperatures stay between the extremes of +60°C and −90°C. Winds circulate warm and cold air round the Earth.

Heat evaporates water from the oceans as a gas called water vapour. This condenses to give cloud, rain and snow. Rivers move the water back to the oceans. Temperatures, winds and rain combine to give the earth's **climates** and daily **weather**.

Figure 3 *The Earth's atmosphere*

Life on Earth

The different climates help give Earth a rich variety of both plant and animal life. The word **biosphere** describes places where there is life. Plants and animals, including people, depend on each other in many ways.

A giant system

Lithosphere, hydrosphere, atmosphere and biosphere combine to give different **environments** (Figure 4). They form part of a **system** in which changes to one bring changes to all the others (Figure 5).

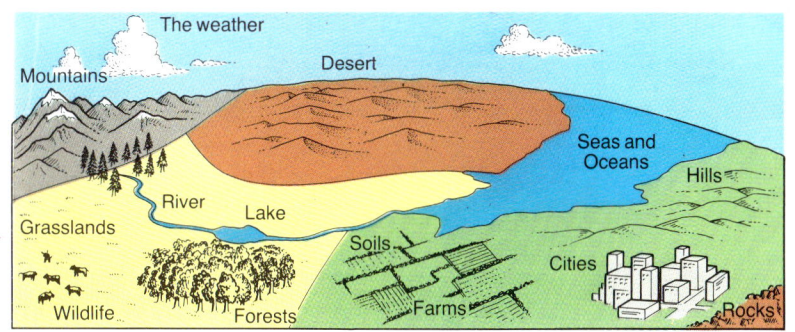

Figure 4 *Parts of the Earth's systems*

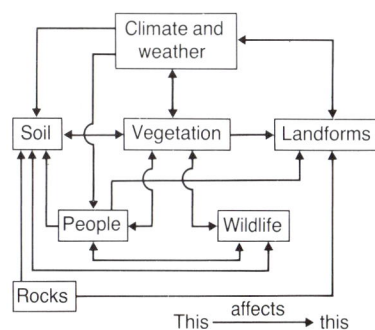

Figure 5 *Links in the system*

Exercises

7   Find atlas maps showing world temperatures and rainfall. Choose three places. Name them and describe how the climate is different in each place.

8   Draw a diagram to show how water moves from the oceans to land, then back again. Label in the words used in the text above.

9   a Make a simple classification of the different types of life on earth. Include the main types of plants and animals.
    b What word describes places where there is life?

10 Write a paragraph to explain Figure 4. Give examples of how one thing affects another.

Minerals make rocks

The crust is made of many types of **rocks**. Rocks are a mixture of separate **minerals** such as quartz (Figure 6). Granite is made of three minerals. These are quartz, feldspar and mica (Figure 7). Minerals make rocks as different as chalk is from coal.

Figure 6 *Minerals: quartz, mica and feldspar*

Figure 7 *A piece of granite*

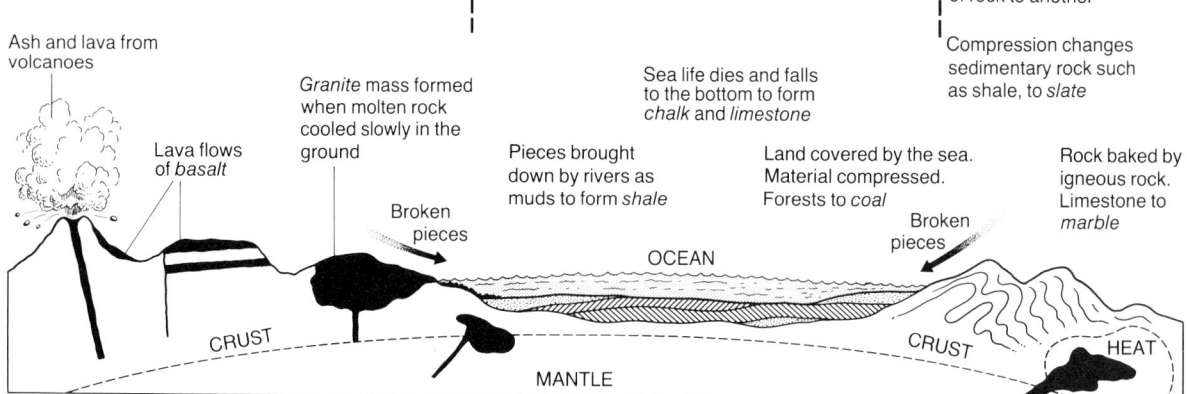

Figure 8 *How rocks are formed*

Types of rock

Rocks are divided into groups depending on how the rock was formed (Figure 8). **Igneous** rocks come from below the crust. **Sedimentary** rocks are formed from pieces of other rocks or ancient life. **Metamorphic** rocks are rocks which have been changed by heat and pressure.

Minerals are broken up and put together many times to form different rocks (Figure 9). This change is called the **rock cycle**.

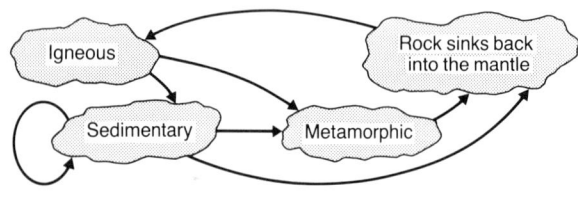

Figure 9 *The rock cycle*

Exercises

11 a Draw a sketch of Figure 7.
    b Add a label to say what it is.
    c What words best describe its shape?
    d Describe how a rock is made of minerals. Use granite or another rock as an example.

12 Study Figure 8. Draw a chart and fill in information about these things.

Type of rock	Examples	How they formed
Igneous	Granite	Cooled slowly in the ground

13 a Draw the rock cycle sketch in Figure 9.
    b Use Figure 8 to explain the diagram.

Lines of weakness

Most rocks have lines of weakness. In sedimentary rocks, **bedding planes** show how the rock was laid down in layers (Figure 10). **Joints** are cracks which occur as a rock dries out or when it bends.

Cracks in igneous rocks are formed as they cool down. They can also form as the weight of overlying rocks is removed by weather, ice and rivers (Figure 11). Cracks appear as the rock is able to expand.

Figure 10 *Sedimentary rocks in the Grand Canyon*

Figure 11 *Joints in igneous rocks*

Rocks and water

Joints and bedding planes allow water to pass through rock. Water can also be held in spaces between grains. A rock that water can pass through is said to be **permeable**. An **impermeable** rock does not let water through.

Rocks and landforms

Rocks vary in hardness. Hard rocks are usually **resistant** to being worn away. They often stand out as distinct shapes or as hills (Figure 12).

The word **relief** describes the slopes and general height of the land. Landscapes are carved into different shapes called **landforms**.

Figure 12 *Ayers Rock: a sandstone outcrop in central Australia*

Exercises

14 a Draw a sketch of Figure 10. Label in:
    the type of rock
    joints and bedding planes
    how the rock was formed

15 Draw three sketches to show these things:
    a Molten rock moving up into the crust
    b Layers of overlying rock worn away
    c Cooled rock expands and joints are formed

16 a Write a definition for:
    permeable rock
    impermeable rock
    b Why are many types of sedimentary rock permeable, such as limestone?

17 Write a paragraph to describe Figure 12. Include these words:
    relief ... landform ... sedimentary ... bedding planes

1.3 Moving plates

Most parts of the Earth's crust are stable. People in some places are not so lucky. They live under threat from volcanoes, earthquakes, landslides and tidal waves.

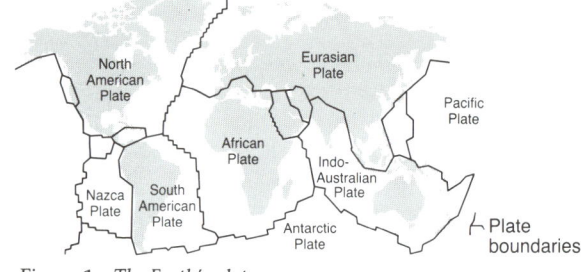

Figure 1   *The Earth's plates*

Floating plates

The crust is the Earth's hard outer shell. It is made of rocks that are lighter than the mantle rocks below. The light crustal rocks 'float' on top of the mantle.

But the shell is not all in one piece. It is divided into large pieces called **plates** (Figure 1).

Types of plate

Some plates are thick with a core of hard rock, such as granite (Figure 2). These make up the main land masses and are called **continental plates**.

Beneath the oceans, there are much thinner plates mainly made of basalt (Figure 3). These are the **oceanic plates**.

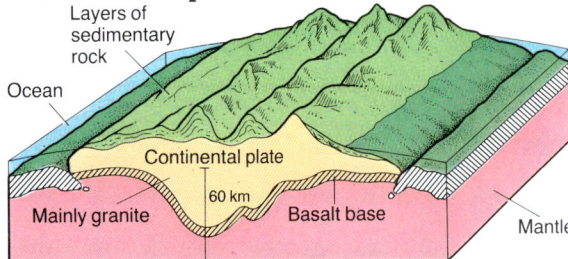

Figure 2   *Continental plates*

> ## *Exercises*
>
> 1   Complete this paragraph with the correct word (either/or):
>   The Earth's crust is divided into sections called shells/plates. The plates are made of rock that is lighter/heavier than material in the core/mantle beneath. The size of each plate is the same/different. The shape of the plates is mainly irregular/circular.
>
> 2   a   Draw Figures 2 and 3.
>   b   List the ways that continental plates are different from oceanic plates. Mention: thickness ... rocks ... relief.

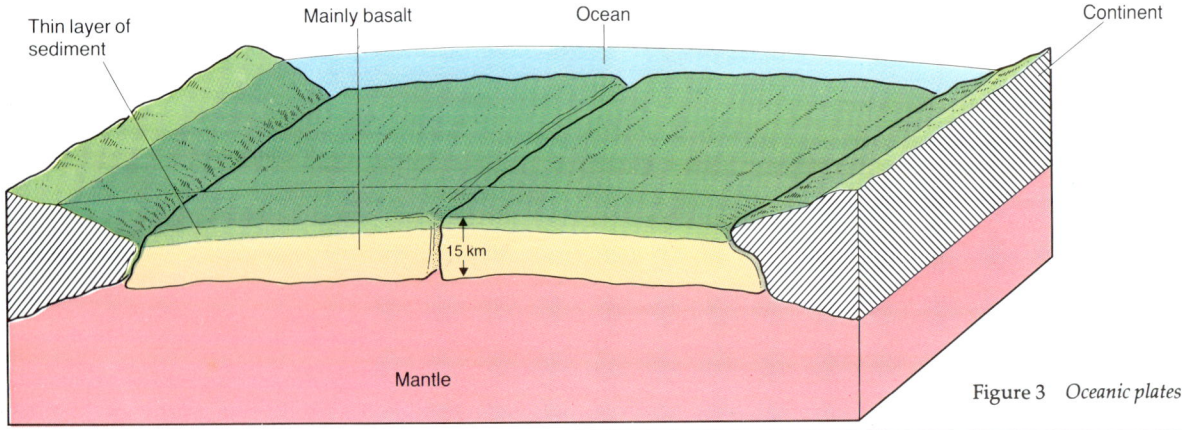

Figure 3   *Oceanic plates*

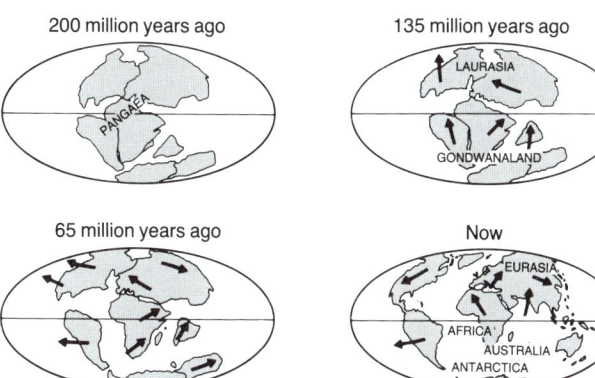

→ Direction of plate movement

Figure 4 *Moving continents*

Jigsaw plates

The plates do not stay in the same place. The continents used to be joined to make one giant **land mass** geologists call Pangaea (Figure 4). Since then the plates have broken apart and moved to where they are now. New oceans have formed and old ones closed up (Figure 5).

The movement is still going on. The North Atlantic widens by about 2 cm each year. Some plates move at up to 10 cm each year.

Dragged along

It seems likely that the plates are dragged along by currents beneath (Figure 6). Rising heat from the core sets up **convection currents** in the mantle rock. The plates are pulled along by molten rock moving in these currents.

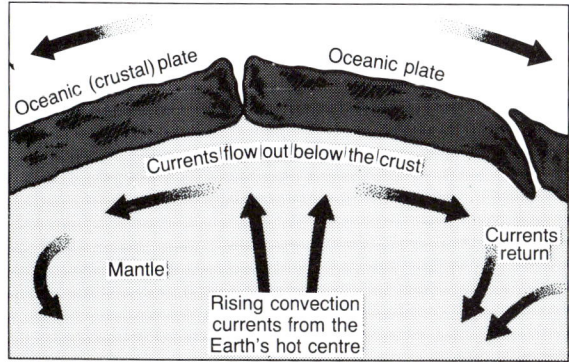

Figure 6 *Convection currents*

Exercises

3
  a Explain the term 'land mass'.
  b How do plate movements help explain the shapes of the continents? Give some examples of places the shapes seem to fit.
  c What evidence might be found near the edges of continents to show they were once joined together? (Hint: rocks and fossils.)
  d Complete this sum to see how far continents can move in 50 million years.

  $$\frac{(2 \text{ cm} \times 50\,000\,000)}{100\,000 \text{ (cm to 1 km)}} = ? \text{ km}$$

  e How do convection currents move plates?

Figure 5 *The Red Sea opening up*

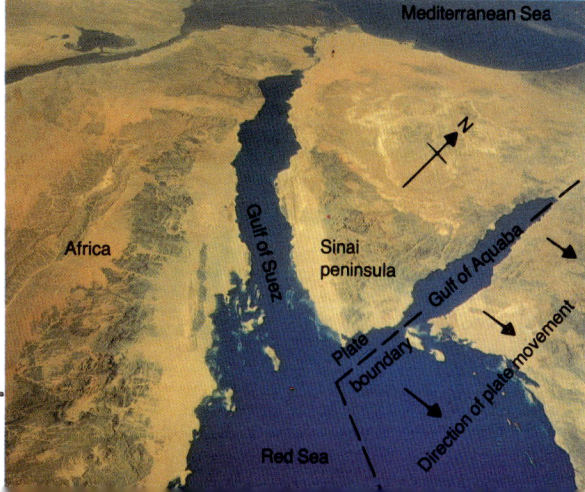

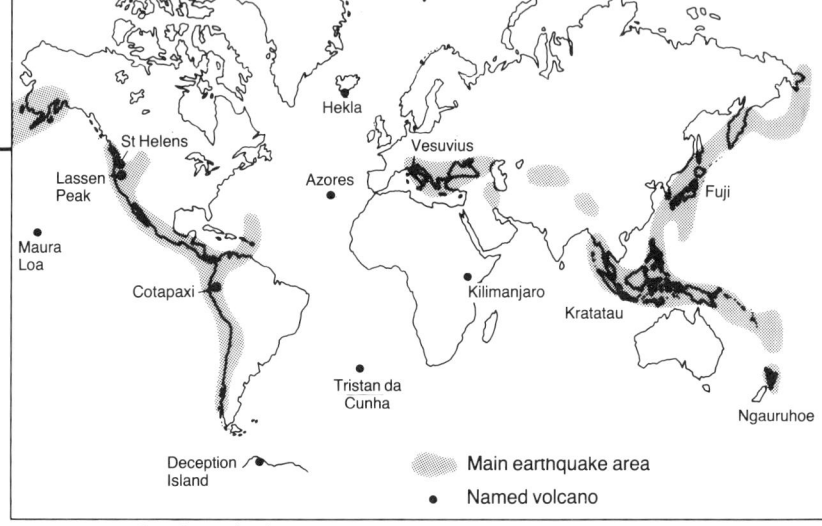

Figure 7 Earthquakes and volcanoes

Stress on the margin

Some plates move towards each other (Figure 7). Others move apart. Plates can also slide past each other heading in opposite directions.

This movement sets up stress at the **plate margin**. The world's **earthquake belts** and volcanoes mainly lie along these plate margins.

Pulling apart

A gap is made where plates pull apart (Figure 8). Molten rock from the mantle moves up to fill the gap. Lava flows out on both sides and forms a **ridge**. This process is called **sea floor spreading**. It makes new plate material along a zone called the **constructive plate margin**.

The lava has an unusual rounded shape and is called **pillow lava** (Figure 9). It oozes out then cools quickly on the sea bed.

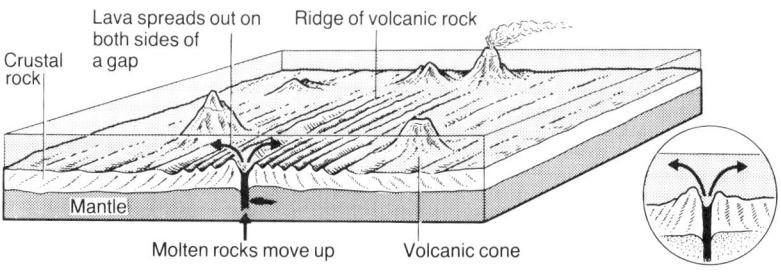

Figure 8 Spreading ridges

Figure 9 Pillow lava

Volcanic lines

In some places, **volcanic cones** build up along the ridge. Some grow to become islands such as Ascension Island in the South Atlantic. Most are completely underwater.

Exercises

4 a Draw diagrams to show the three directions in which plates can move.
   b How does a map of earthquake belts and volcanoes help show where plate margins are? Name some places as examples.
   c Explain the term 'sea floor spreading'.
   d Name some places that are free from major earthquakes or volcanoes? Explain why.

5 a Make a sketch to show pillow lava.
   b Add labels to describe and explain:
      what it is made of
      its shape
      where it was formed
      why it was formed

6 a Explain why there is a ridge in mid-Atlantic.
   b Explain the location of Ascension Island.

Plate destruction

When plates move towards each other, one plate rides over the other forcing it down into the mantle (Figure 10). Rock is melted in the mantle and the plate is destroyed. This area is called the **destructive plate margin**.

Trenches, earthquakes and volcanoes

The deep ocean **trenches** are along the destructive plate margins. This is also the zone where earthquakes are most common. Vibrations occur as plates meet and rock is melted.

Molten rock from a plate is lighter than the rock around it in the mantle (Figure 11). It forces its way up through cracks as **magma**, and erupts as volcanoes.

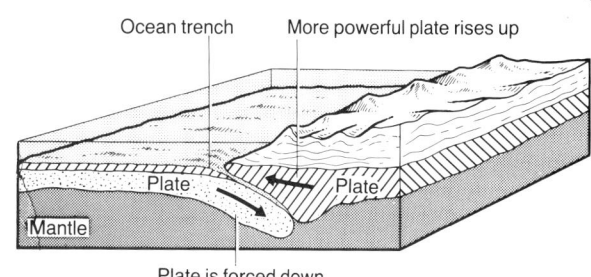

Figure 10 *Destructive plate margins*

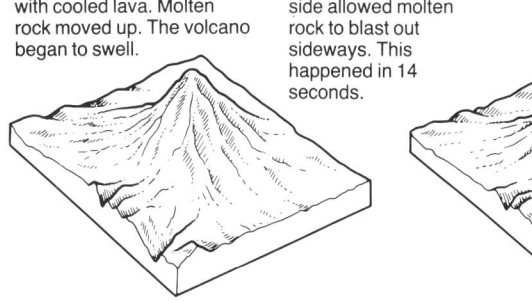

Figure 11 *Volcanoes and plates*

Blowing its top

The most violent volcanic eruptions are usually in areas where plates come together.

Magma forces its way up through lines of weakness under great pressure. This is often into the base of an existing volcano where the vent is blocked with hardened lava (Figure 12).

The whole top may be blown off to form a **caldera**.

Figure 12 *St. Helens erupts*

Exercises

7 a Make a copy of Figure 10.
   b Add notes to explain why:
      one plate is forced downwards
      the plate is destroyed

8 Use an atlas to name and give the depth of some trenches in the Pacific Ocean.

9 a Explain the link between destructive plate margins and volcanoes.
   b What causes violent volcanic eruptions?
   c Use Figure 12 to describe the St. Helens eruption.
   d Draw sketches to show a caldera being formed. The whole top should be blown off!

1.4 Structures and landforms

The Earth's crust is crinkled with hills and mountains, plateaus and plains. These features are pushed up then carved into shape. They last for a few million years, then are removed again almost without trace.

Figure 1 *Folded rocks*

Rock structures

Sedimentary rocks are usually laid down in horizontal layers called **strata**. This can be on ocean beds or in lowland depressions.

As the Earth's plates move, these layers become bent and broken into new shapes (Figure 1). The pattern made by a rock strata is called a **structure**.

A folded structure

Pressure from both sides can buckle the strata into **folds** (Figure 2). These can be on any scale from small ripples to structures measuring thousands of metres.

The top part of a fold is called an **anticline**. The bottom part is a **syncline**.

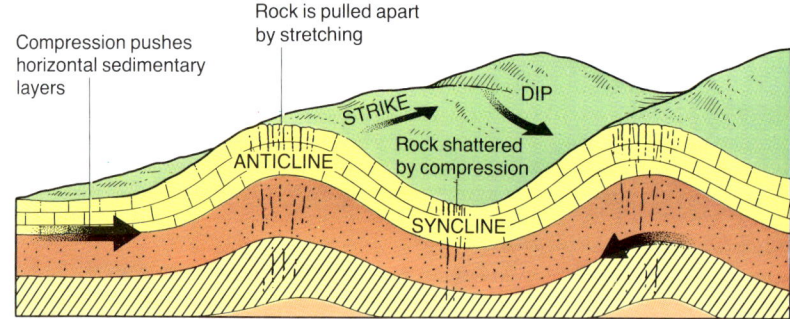

Figure 2 *An anticline and a syncline*

Relief and structure

The surface of structures such as anticlines are worn down over time (Figure 3). The relief changes, but the rocks below still have their original structure.

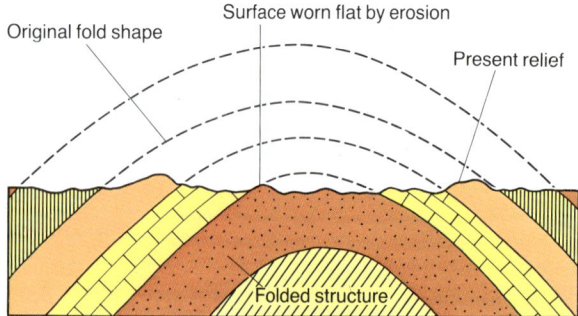

Figure 3 *An eroded anticline*

Exercises

1 Make a copy of Figure 2.

2 a Why are sedimentary rocks built up in layers?
   b Describe what has happened to the strata in Figure 1.
   c What causes rocks to be folded?
   d Why is rock weakened at the top of an anticline and the base of a syncline?

3 Describe the geological history of the rocks in Figure 3. Use these words:
   strata ... fold ... anticline ... structure.

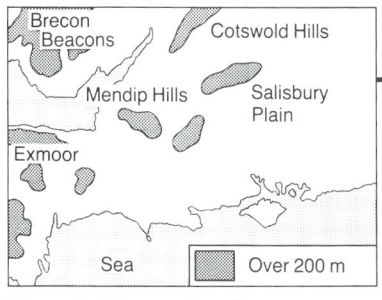
Figure 4 The Mendip Hills

The Mendip fold

The Mendip Hills in Somerset have a folded structure (Figure 4). Layers of limestone and sandstone have been folded up (Figure 5). The limestone on top has been worn away (Figure 6). The older sandstone beneath now shows through to form the highest land (Figure 7).

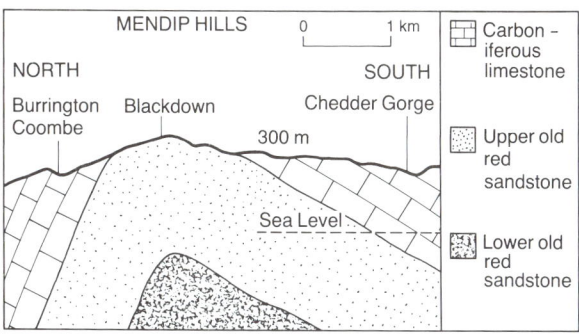
Figure 5 Mendip geological cross-section

Figure 6 The Mendip structure

Types of folding

There are different types of fold (Figure 8). Some are pushed over in mainly one direction. Others are completely folded over until the layers of rock are upside down.

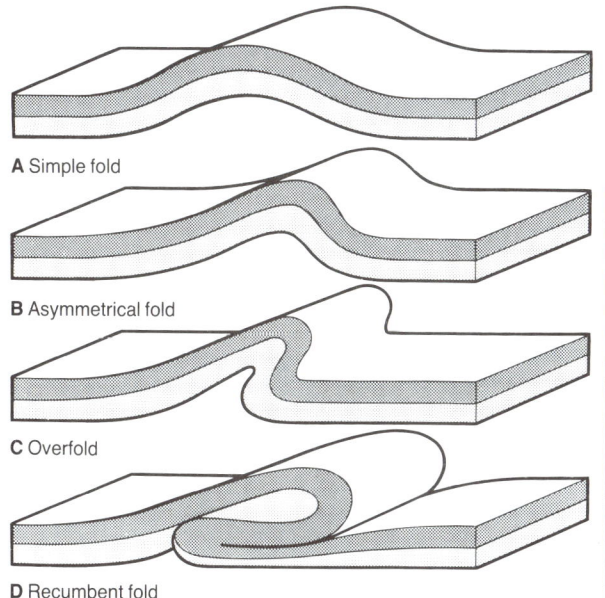
Figure 8 Types of folds

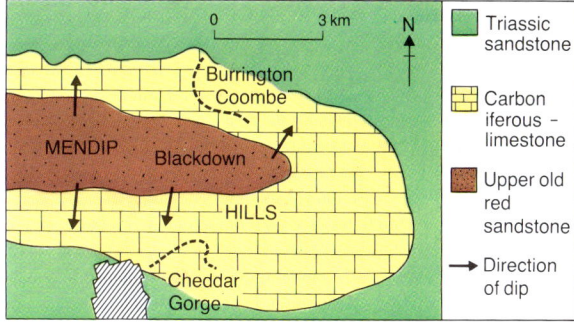
Figure 7 Mendip geology map

Exercises

4 Use Figure 6 and an atlas to describe the relief and structure of the Mendip Hills.

5 a What is the name given to the Mendip structure?
   b Explain why the oldest rocks are on the top of the hills.

6 Describe and draw the different types of fold. Why do these differences occur?

Mountain ranges

Most mountain ranges have been formed by folding (Figure 9). Sedimentary rocks in ocean beds have been compressed and pushed up. The Himalayas are still rising as the plates continue to move.

Plates and mountains

Oceans disappeared as plates moved together (Figure 10). Ocean sediments have been squeezed up into giant folds. The **fossil** remains of sea creatures can be found on mountain peaks.

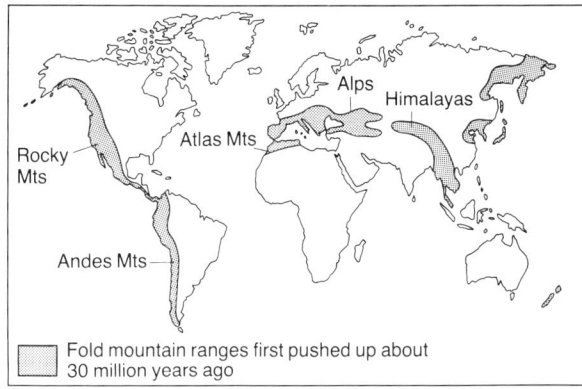

Figure 9 *Major fold mountain ranges*

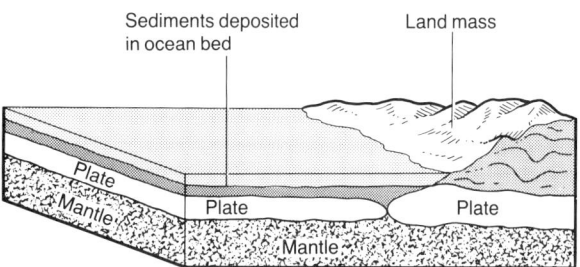

Figure 10 *How fold mountains are formed*

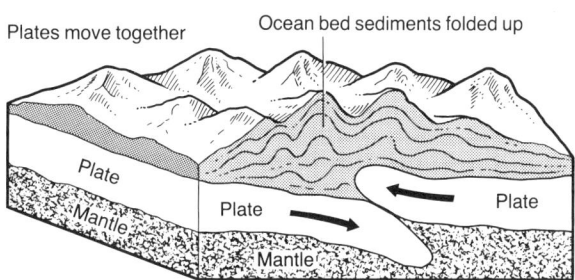

The high Andes

The Andes mountains are being formed as two plates move together (Figure 11). Volcanoes erupt as molten material from the melting Nazca plate forces its way up to the surface. In 1985, the Nevado del Ruiz volcano in Colombia erupted causing a mud flow which killed thousands of people. Earthquakes are an added hazard in this area. In the same year, earthquakes in Chile caused widespread damage and death.

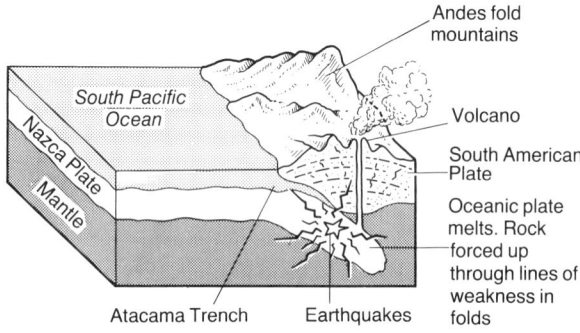

Figure 11 *The Andes mountains*

Exercises

7 Shade in the main fold mountain ranges on a world outline. Use an atlas to find the highest peaks in each range. Mark them in.

8 What evidence of folding would you expect to find on the tops of mountains such as the Alps? (Hint: structure, rock type, fossils.)

9 Use an atlas to draw a map of the Andes mountain range. Add notes about these things:
   distances north to south and east to west
   heights and relief
   the Andes folded structure
   the Atacama Trench
   earthquakes and volcanoes
   the direction of plate movements

British Isles mountains

There are no really high mountains in the British Isles. Ben Nevis is the highest at 1344 m, which is many times smaller than peaks in the Alps or Himalayas.

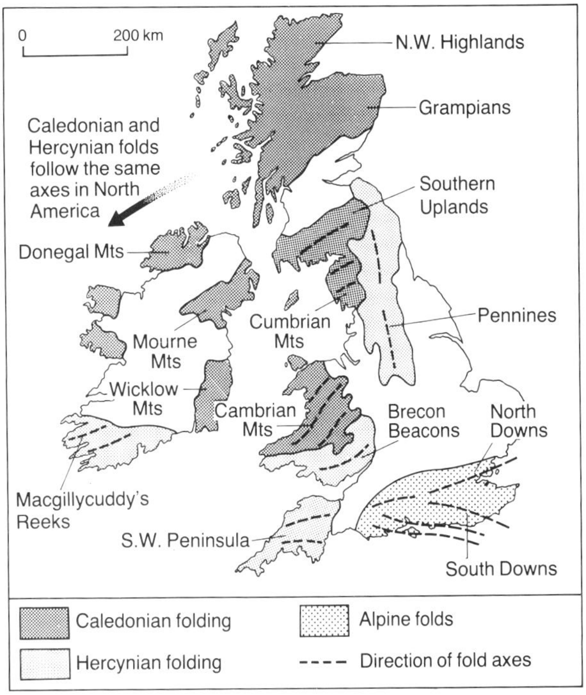

Past folding

The Alps and Himalayas were folded about 30 million years ago. The British mountains are very much older (Figure 12). Some were first folded about 400 million years ago. This was during a mountain building period known as the Caledonian **orogeny**.

During the Hercynian orogeny 280 million years ago, mountains were formed in south west Britain. Some of the older structures were refolded at the same time.

Some folding took place while the Alps were being formed. This was fairly gentle and mostly in the south east.

Figure 12 *British Isles mountains*

Snowdon's story

Snowdon, in North Wales, is 1085 m high. It is part of an ancient folded structure that once formed a much higher mountain range (Figure 13). The higher peaks have been worn down. Snowdon is the remnant of the base of a fold.

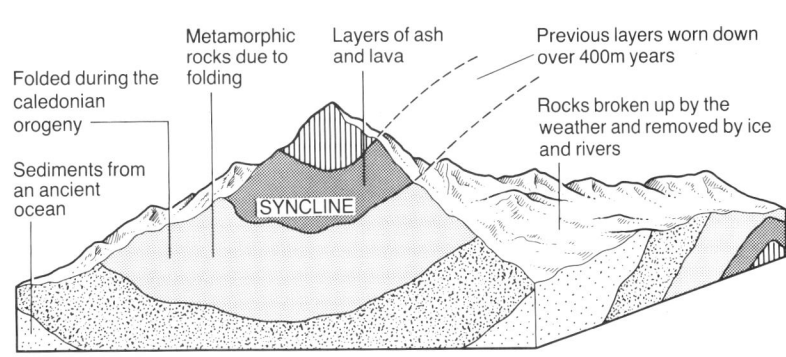

Figure 13 *Structure and rocks of Snowdon*

Exercises

10 On an outline of the British Isles, shade in and name the main mountain ranges. Use an atlas. Name the highest peak in each range and say what height it is.

11 a What is an orogeny?
    b List the three orogenies with their dates.

12 a What do each of these things tell you about the geological history of Snowdon?
       it is mainly made of metamorphic rocks
       there are deposits of volcanic rock
       the structure is a syncline
       there are several other peaks of about the same height nearby
    b What is continually wearing away and changing the shape of Snowdon?

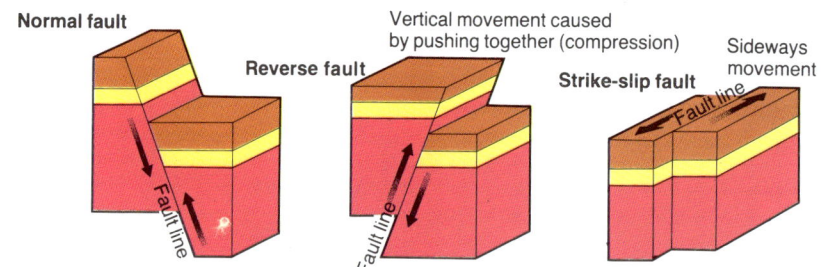

Figure 14 *Types of faulting*

Breaking point

Layers of rock can bend, up to a point. Then there is a break. A break in the strata is called a **fault**.

A fault can be caused by tension pulling the rock apart (Figure 14). This gives a **normal fault**. Pushing together from either side gives a **reverse fault**. A **tear fault** is when the movement is sideways.

Fault lines

A long steep slope called an **escarpment** can be formed along a **fault line** (Figure 15). One side of the fault is pushed up. In time, the escarpment wears back from the original fault (Figure 16).

Finding faults

New faulting is most common along plate margins where an earth tremor or more serious quake may be felt. Some faults continue to move long after they were first formed. The effects of this are seldom serious or even noticed.

Figure 15 *The fault escarpment at Ochil, Stirlingshire*

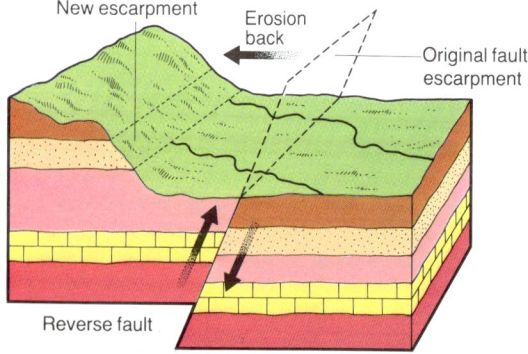

Figure 16 *An eroded fault escarpment*

Exercises

13 a What would you see if rock strata had a fault line?
   b What landform may be caused along a normal or reverse fault?
   c How is a strike-slip fault different from other types of fault?
   d Explain how the direction of pressure gives different types of fault.

14 Make a sketch of Figure 15. Add notes about:
   the names of the landforms
   size and angle of slopes
   how the feature may change (see Figure 16)

Large scale features

In the Rocky Mountains in Nevada USA, faulting has given areas of flat-topped **plateaus** and low flat land called **basins** (Figure 17). This is known as **block faulting**. Rocks have been thrown both up and down to form this landscape.

Death Valley

Death Valley is the hottest and driest part of the USA (Figure 18). The land has dropped down along fault lines between block mountains on either side (Figure 19). A valley formed in this way is called a **rift valley**. The steep fault-line slopes can still be clearly seen (Figure 20).

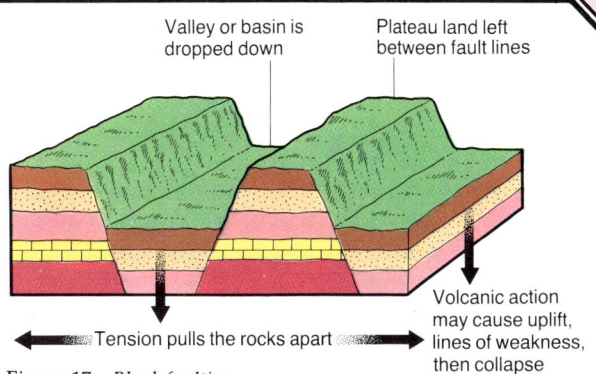

Figure 17 *Block faulting*

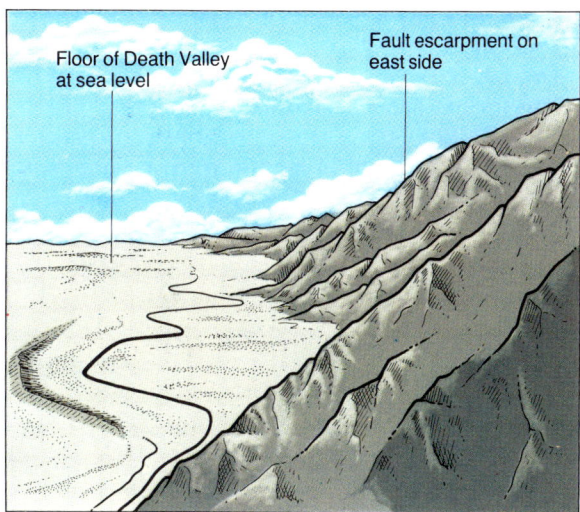

Figure 20 *Death Valley escarpment*

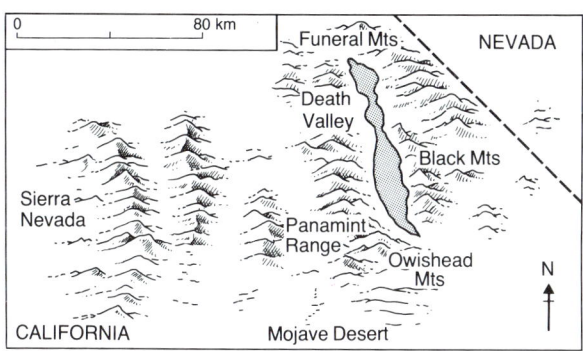

Figure 18 *Plateau land in Nevada*

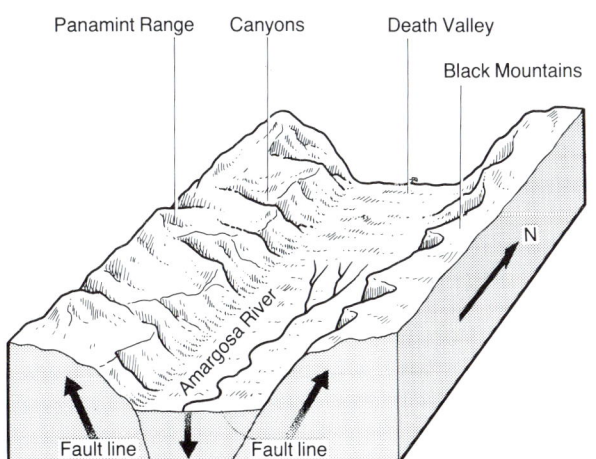

Figure 19 *The Death Valley rift*

Exercises

15 Study Figure 17.
   a What kind of movement has caused faulting?
   b How have the valleys and basins been formed?

16 What evidence is there on Figures 17, 18 and 19 that Death Valley has been formed by faulting? Mention:
   the valley size and shape
   surrounding mountains
   the geological structure
   the valley slopes

1.5 Geology in action

People have used rocks since the stone age. Today, even nuclear power comes from uranium in rocks.

Rocks and resources

Rocks are the raw materials for building and making things (Figure 1). Some can be used straight from a quarry, such as granite. Rocks which have a metal are called **ores**. The ore, such as iron, is melted out in a furnace.

Rocks also give power. Coal and oil are the two main types. These are called **fossil fuels**.

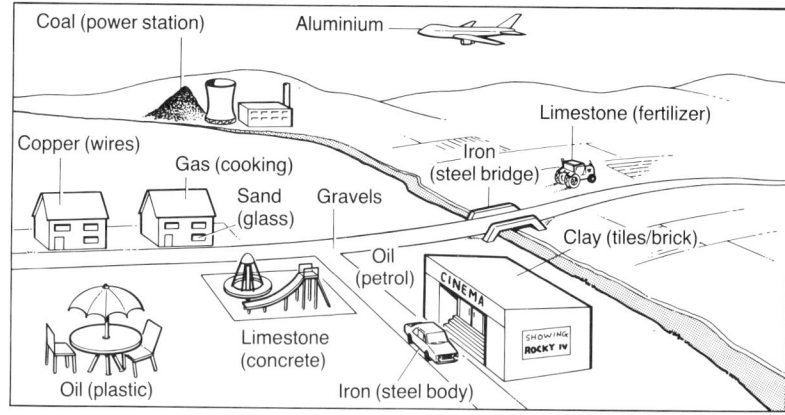

Figure 1 *Rocks and resources*

Britain's rock resources

Britain has many types of metal ores and other useful rocks (Figure 2). Metals are in old metamorphic rocks but most **deposits** are too small to be worth mining.

The coalfields are where tropical forests grew in swampy conditions 350 million years ago. Coal is used to produce 80 per cent of Britain's electricity.

Younger rocks are mainly clays and limestones. These are made into bricks and cement.

Exercises

1 a What is an ore?
   b What is a fossil fuel?

2 Use Figure 1 to describe the importance of rocks. Give examples using these headings:
   a Transport
   b Power
   c Building
   d Farming

3 Give examples to show the variety of Britain's mineral resources. Say why they are not all mined.

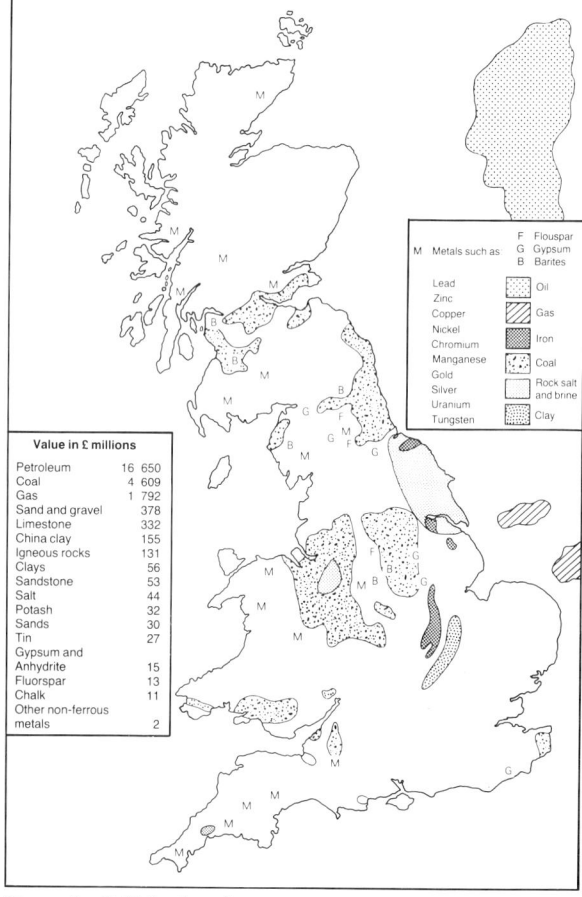

Figure 2 *British mineral resources*

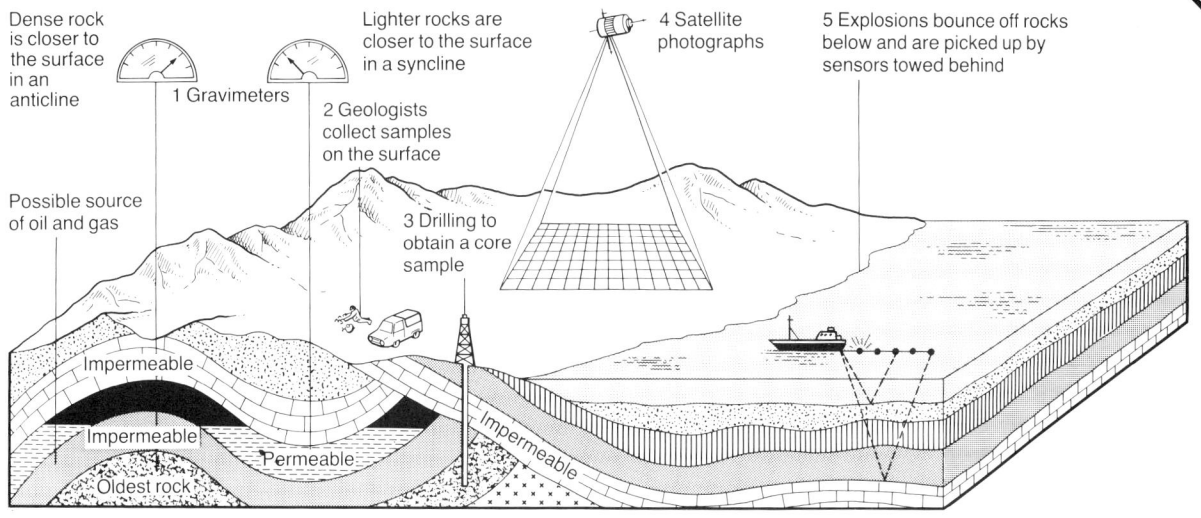

Figure 3 *Structure and minerals*

Structures and mining

People need to know about the rock structure before they begin mining. If there are faults, mining may be too difficult and expensive.

A map of structures can be made by **seismic survey** (Figure 3). Vibrations are sent into the rocks either by shaking or by explosions. The vibrations are recorded as they bounce at different speeds from different rock types.

Gravity in the rocks can also be measured to show structures. It is higher in an anticline because older more dense rocks are near the surface.

Satellite images

Satellite photographs are used to identify rocks and structures. This is especially useful in areas which are difficult to get to.

Core geology

The only sure way to find out what is below ground is by boring a hole. A **core sample** is brought up so geologists can study the rocks at first hand (Figure 4).

Figure 4 *Studying core samples*

Exercises

4 What methods would you use to find out about the geological structure in these places, and what information would each method give you?
  a Under the sea
  b A remote mountain area
  c A lowland plain
  Give reasons for your answers.

5 Draw a diagram to show the structures where oil is most likely to be found.

6 What can a core sample tell about the rocks?

21

California on the move

California is in earthquake country (Figure 5). The San Andreas fault line divides two of the Earth's plates. Land west of the fault is moving north. To the east it is moving south.

The danger zones

The plates move an average of 3.5 cm a year (Figure 6). This is only an average. The danger points are where the plates are locked together (Figure 7). Tension builds up at these points. Rocks bend under the strain, there is a sudden jerk, the strain is released and the land moves violently.

Earthquake forecast

Geologists in California record about 10 000 earth movements a year. They are mostly unnoticed as they are below magnitude (M) 2 on the **Richter Scale**. The problem is predicting when the next big earthquake will come (Figure 8).

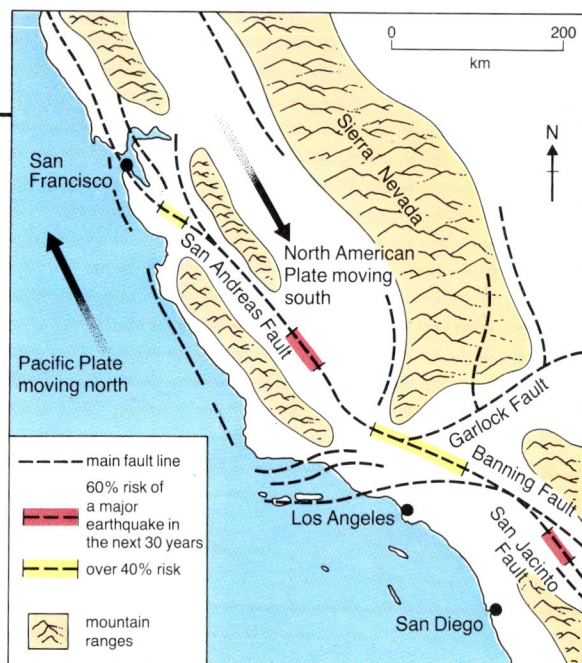

Figure 5 *Earthquake areas in California*

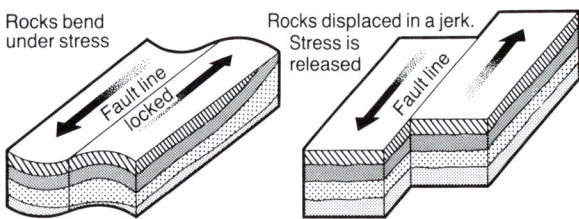

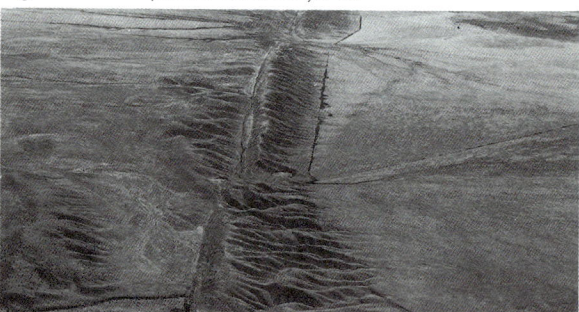

Figure 6 *The San Andreas fault line*

Figure 7 *The causes of an earthquake*
Figure 8 *Predicting earthquakes*

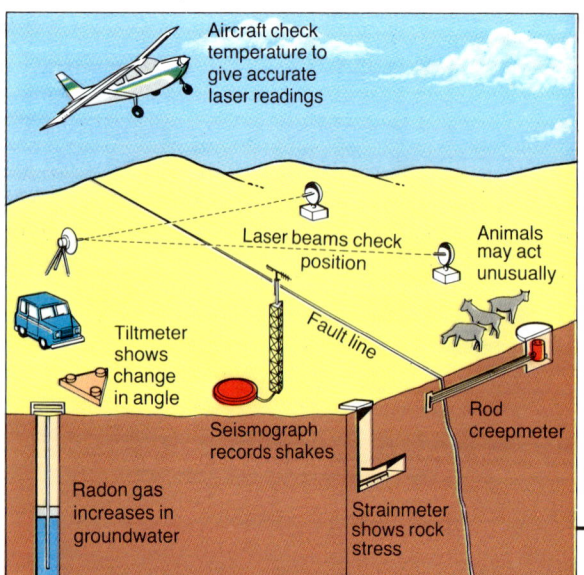

Exercises

6 Use Figure 5 and an atlas to draw a large map of California to show these things:
   the San Andreas and other fault lines
   mountains and rivers
   settlement and communications

7 a Which of the three types of fault is the San Andreas?
   b On average, how far does the land move in 50 years?
   c Explain why some places along the fault are more likely to have large earthquakes than others.
   d Describe the methods being used to predict when earthquakes will occur.

Earthquake effects

An earthquake above M5 can be very destructive even though it lasts less than a minute (Figure 9). Buildings become unsafe and collapse. Gas and electricity lines are broken and this can cause fires. Water mains and sewers can also be broken, causing health problems.

Plans for protection

Some precautions are being taken to reduce earthquake damage. No more houses will be built along the fault line (Figure 10). Old buildings are being replaced in the most risky areas. Tall buildings will not be built near the fault. People are being taught how to take precautions in the home (Figure 11).

Figure 9 *Emergency earthquake drill in a school*

Taming earthquakes

Scientists and engineers are trying to prevent serious earthquakes happening. They pump water into the fault to lubricate places where it is locked. Underground explosions might even help. In the meantime, better means of prediction seems to be the best way to avoid disasters.

Safety at home
—Secure gas and other pipes
—Do not put heavy objects on high shelves
—Have earthquake drills for practice

Emergency stores
— Torch with batteries
— Canned food
— First aid box

After the earthquake
—Keeps away from fallen power lines
—Check sewers before flushing toilets
—Use phone only in an emergency
—Be ready for more shocks

During an earthquake
—Get under a table
—Stay away from windows

Figure 10 *Homes in danger near San Francisco*

Figure 11 *Safety in the home*

Exercises

8 Invent a short newspaper report to describe a major earthquake in California. Give your newspaper a name and include a headline, drawing, technical details and account of the damage.

9 a What mistake has been made in planning land use in Figure 10?

   b Give examples of land use that would be more suitable near the fault line.

10 Design a sheet or leaflet to give practical advice to people who live in areas where earthquakes are likely.

11 Do you think that earthquakes can ever be controlled along the fault?

Antarctic minerals

Information about plate movements is being used to find minerals in Antarctica. Geologists believe that a giant continent they call Gondwana began to break up 170 million years ago (Figure 12). Iron ore and other minerals are already mined in the parts of South America and Australia nearest to Antarctica. If the Gondwana idea is true, the same deposits may also be found in Antarctica (Figure 13).

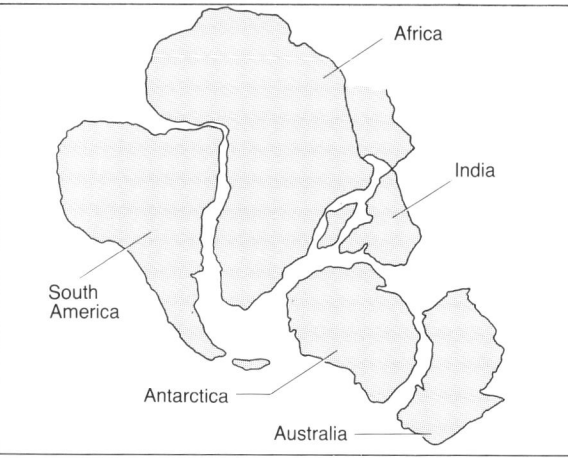

Figure 12 *The continents break up*

Past climates

Coal has also been found in Antarctica (Figure 14). This shows that the continent was once where the climate was much warmer. Now most of it is under 2000 m of ice.

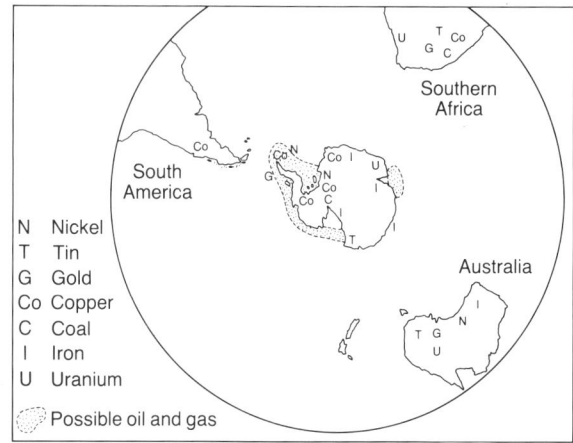

Figure 13 *Minerals in Antarctica*

Figure 14 *Coal seams in Antarctica*

Oil basins

Exploration is taking place to find oil and gas. These may be found in sedimentary basins on Antarctica's continental shelf. These basins were formed after Gondwana broke up. Seismic surveys and drilling are needed to get more information. The thick moving pack ice makes this very difficult.

Exercises

12 a In what main way is Antarctica different from areas around the North Pole?
   b What proof would you look for to see if the Gondwana continent ever existed?
   c How could you find out the date when the continent began to break up?
   d What does Figure 14 show about the rocks of Antarctica?

13 a What makes mineral exploration and mining so difficult in Antarctica?
   b Why might oil resources be exploited first? (Hint: value and scarcity.)
   c Some people do not want any resources to be exploited in Antarctica. Why do you think this is so? (Hint: conservation.)

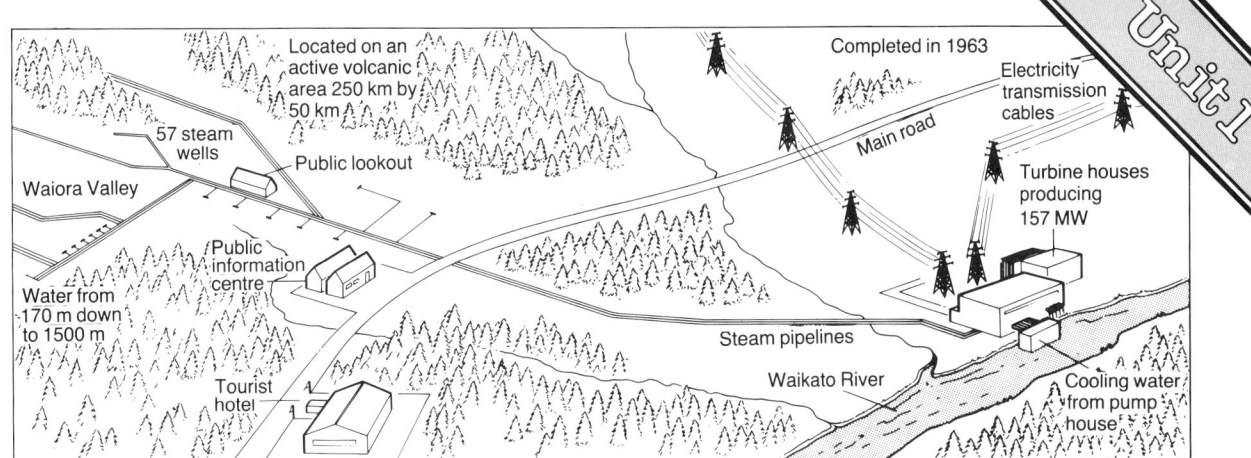

Figure 15 *The Wairakei Geothermal Power Station*

Getting up steam

Underground water becomes heated when in close contact with hot rocks. When this water reaches the surface, pressure is released, the water boils and turns to a jet of steam. This is how a **geyser** works (Figure 16). Geysers are mainly found in areas where there are active volcanoes.

Power from down under

In New Zealand, this steam is being used to drive turbines and give electricity (Figure 15). This type of energy is called **geothermal** power as it uses the Earth's natural heat (Figure 17).

Figure 16 *A geyser in New Zealand*

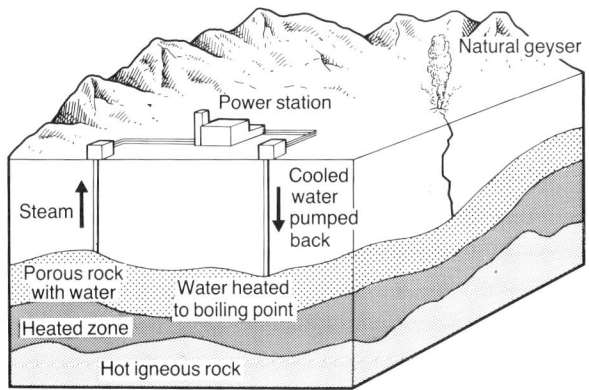

Figure 17 *Steam from below ground*

Never ending power

Once used, the steam is cooled and turned back into water. The water is injected back into the rocks so that pressure is kept up and the supply of water does not run out.

Exercises

14 Draw a diagram with labels to show how a geyser erupts. Look at Figure 16.

15 Study Figures 15 and 17.
  a Name the power station. When was it built and say where it is?
  b Why is this a good place for a geothermal power station? (Hint: igneous rocks.)
  c Why is the power station built near a river?
  d Why is this a clean type of power?

16 a What facilities have been provided for visitors at Wairakei?
  b Why do you think tourists want to visit a power station?

The mining business

About 20 000 people work in the South Wales coalmining industry (Figure 18). Their jobs depend on mining coal at a profit. This means selling coal for more than the cost of mining it. Doing this is becoming harder every year (Figure 19). Unprofitable pits are said to be 'uneconomic' and are closed down.

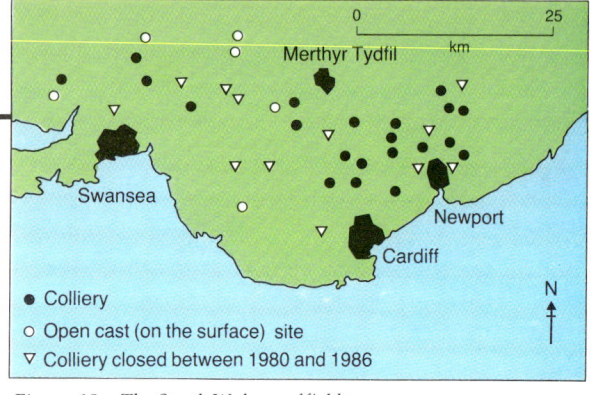

Figure 18 *The South Wales coalfield*

Seams faulted and split

Coal began to be formed in the Carboniferous era about 350 million years ago. Since then, the rocks in South Wales have been severely folded and faulted. Coal **seams** such as the one in Figure 20 are too costly to mine.

Seams sometimes split so that the coal becomes too thin to be worth mining (Figure 21). Cutting machinery that costs between £1 million and £4 million is not worth using on seams like these.

Year	Number of pits	Millions of tonnes mined	People employed in thousands
1970	54	11.3	71
1978	37	7.8	51
1982	35	7.5	46
1986	18	6.5	20

Note: Figures are for National Coal Board mines only. Opencast pits are mined under contract by private companies to give 1.9m tonnes in 1986.

Figure 19 *South Wales coalmining statistics*

Source: South Wales Geology Report from N.C.B.

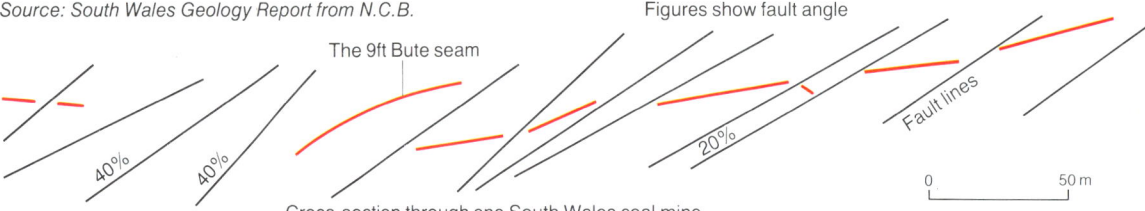

Figure 20 *Faulted coal seams*

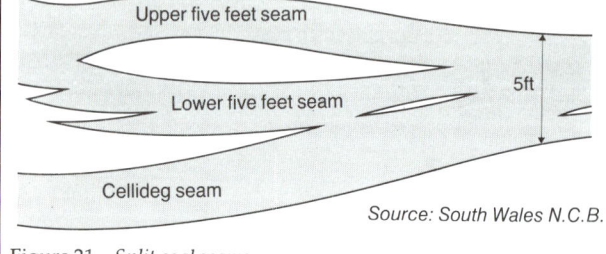

Source: South Wales N.C.B.

Figure 21 *Split coal seams*

Exercises

17 Describe some of the uses of coal. Think about domestic, industrial and energy.

18 Use an atlas to describe the kind of landscape in the South Wales coalfield area.

19 a How have the number of coal mines and the amount of coal being mined changed since 1970?
    b How many jobs were lost in coalmining between 1970 and 1986?
    c What problems can be caused when 'uneconomic' pits are closed down?

20 Study Figures 20 and 21.
    a Write a geology report to describe the problems there would be in mining the Bute seam.
    b Why can splitting cause problems?

UNIT 2 Breaking the surface

2.1 Introduction

Nothing lasts for ever. In Edinburgh, even the marble gravestones are breaking up at a rate of over 1 mm every 10 years.

Surfaces under attack

All objects in the open air are attacked by the weather. Cars rust and corrode, roads become pitted and buildings decay. Frost, heating and cooling, and chemical action by rain water are the processes which cause this decay. Breaking up the earth's surface by the weather is called **weathering**.

Figure 1 *Weathered dog statue*

A matter of time

The effects of weathering are seen on buildings such as churches (Figure 1). Parts of St. Paul's are crumbling at the rate of 8 to 14 mm a century. Weathering happens slowly, but the dates on gravestones record how effective this process can be (Figure 2).

Soil is formed

Most parts of the land are covered by a layer of broken up rock called the **regolith**. The top layer of the regolith is the **soil**. Weathering plays a major role in forming soils.

The soil in Figure 3 has developed from clay rocks. The stones will eventually break down to form a soil.

Figure 2 *Weathered gravestone*

Figure 3 *Soil profile*

> ## Exercise
> 1 a What is weathering?
>   b Give an example from everyday life.
>   c Describe what has happened to the gravestone in Figure 2. Mention the time it has taken.
>   d Describe what the weather has done in Figure 3.

2.2 Weather at work

Nature works slowly but continually to break up the earth's surface. Some landscapes were made by the weather thousands of years ago.

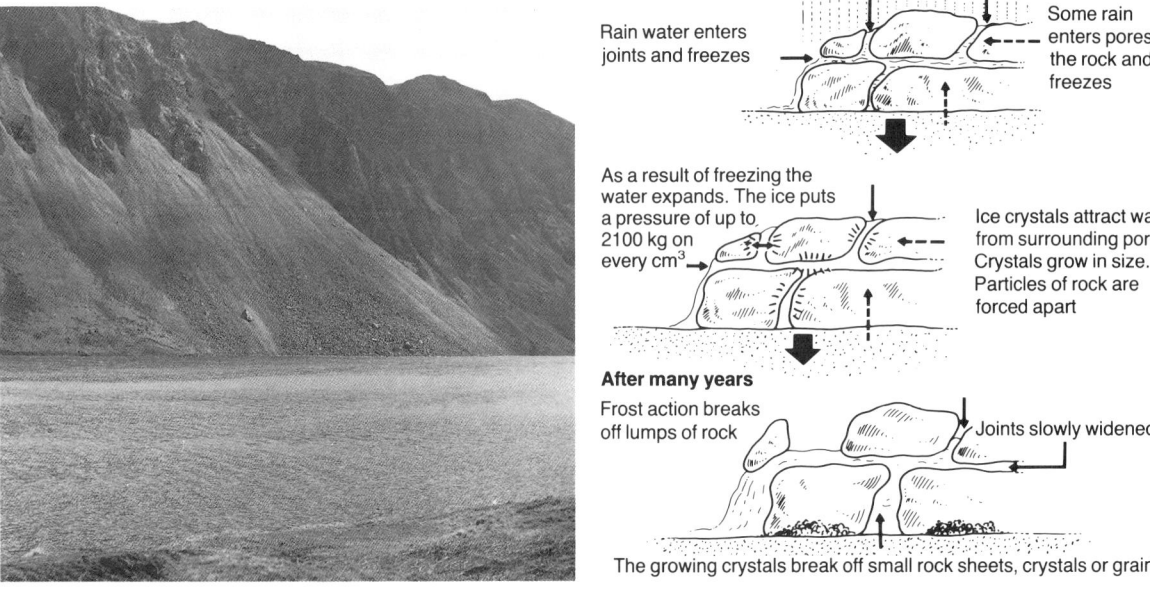

Figure 1 Screes

Figure 2 Frost weathering

Fragmented by frost

Piles of boulders called **screes** often lie at the foot of steep mountain slopes. They have been broken off the cliffs above by frost (Figure 1).

Frost weathering is widespread in high land where there is plenty of moisture and frequent freezing and thawing (Figure 2).

Exposed to the elements

Some rocks begin to break up when they are **exposed** on the surface for the first time. Igneous rocks, for example, are often formed 20 km or more underground. As the covering rocks are stripped off by **erosion**, the igneous rocks may be split by horizontal cracks called **pressure release** jointing (Figure 3).

Figure 3 Pressure release jointing in granite

The type of rock

Different rocks are affected by weathering in different ways. Shales and clays are weak rocks. They can be weathered by wetting and drying. They expand when wet but shrink when they dry out. These stresses weaken the rocks and make them break up (Figure 4).

Joints and bedding planes are ready-made lines of weaknesses. They open up more rock to attack (Figure 5).

Figure 4 *Clay which has dried out*

Loosened by life

Animals and plants help to loosen the surface. By burrowing, digging and digesting, rabbits, moles, ants and worms 'weather' the rock (Figure 6). Growing tree roots prise open bigger cracks (Figure 7).

Mechanical weathering

Frost shattering, pressure release and wetting and drying are all types of **mechanical weathering**. The rock is broken up but not changed chemically.

Figure 5 *Shale*

Falling trees can shift 0.25 tonnes with their roots.
Marble gravestones weather at 200 mm in 1000 years.
Ants rework the top 6 cm once every 100–300 years.
Ant hills cover 1–4% of an area.

Figure 6 *Weathering statistics*

Exercises

1. Use Figure 2 to describe how the screes in Figure 1 were formed.

2. How were the cracks made in Figure 3?

3. Why are the following rocks easy to weather?
    Clay
    Shale

4. Make a sketch to show how living things break up the earth's surface.

5. What is meant by mechanical weathering?

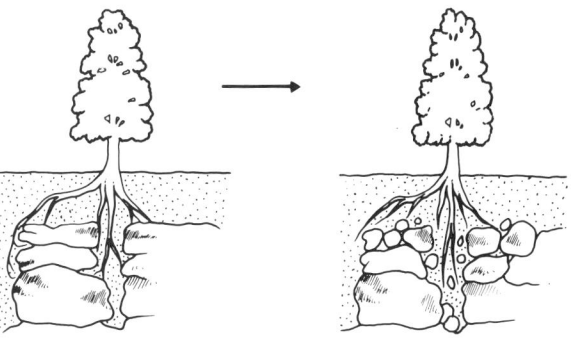

Figure 7 *Tree root weathering*

Rotting rocks

Chemical weathering is the main way rock is broken down. It breaks down granite four times faster than mechanical weathering.

Chemical weathering attacks rock minerals by changing them into other substances. An example is when silicate minerals in igneous rocks break down into clays. The rocks crumble in a process called **granular disintegration**.

Climate	Location	Rock	Weathering loss in mm/1000 years
Tropical rainforest	Aldabra Islands	Limestone	260 (average)
Temperate maritime (like UK)	Belgium	Limestone	2.5 (average)
Tropical rainforest	Malaysia	Mudstone	3.0
Temperate maritime	Wales	Mudstone	1.5

Figure 8 *Tropical weathering statistics*

Moisture at work

Moisture is needed for chemical weathering to take place. The main process is **hydrolysis**. In this process, water reacts with the rock minerals. It is more potent when abundant vegetation and soil organisms make the water more acidic.

In tropical countries, high temperatures, heavy rainfall and luxuriant vegetation give rapid **tropical weathering** (Figure 8). Great depths of weathered rock are formed.

Figure 9 *An inselberg*

Island hills

In the tropical grasslands of Africa steep-sided hills rise from the plains like islands in a sea. The hills are **inselbergs** (Figure 9).

Millions of years ago the land was deeply weathered. Where the rock was more resistant and joints more widely spaced a mound of solid rock was left (Figure 10). Eventually erosion and weathering stripped off the weathered layers and exposed the mounds as inselbergs.

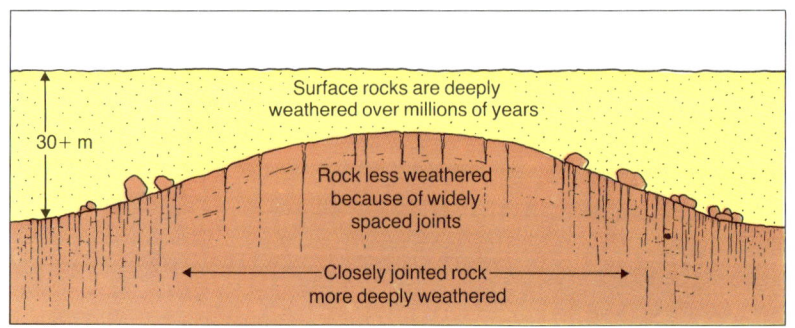

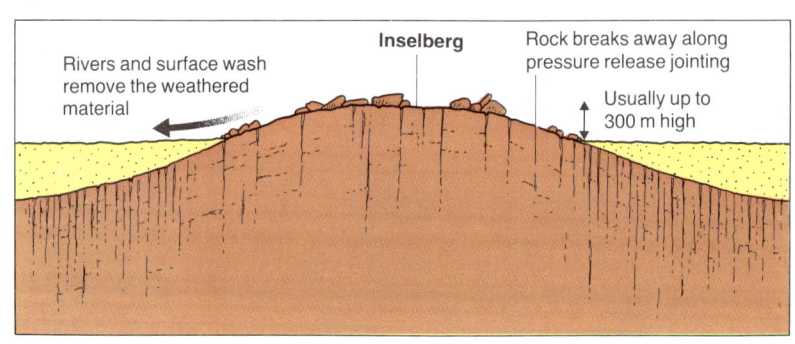

Figure 10 *How an inselberg is formed*

Desert dew

In deserts rocks can be honeycombed by chemical weathering (Figure 11). These **tafoni** are formed where moisture gathers, such as dew and run-off.

Dissolving away

Limestones are weathered by **solution**. This means they are dissolved by water. Rain water absorbs carbon dioxide from the air to form a weak carbonic acid. The acidic water makes solution easier. The limestone is pitted by **solution weathering**. Running water etches out grooves called **karren** (Figure 12).

Figure 11 *Tafoni*

Figure 12 *Limestone karren*

Figure 13 *Weathered conglomerate rock*

Exercises

6 What is the main way rock is broken down?

7 Use Figure 8 to show that weathering is more rapid in the tropics than in the UK.

8 a Make a labelled sketch of Figure 9.
  b Explain how the inselberg was formed. Use Figure 10 and these words:
    granular disintegration ... hydrolysis.

9 Why is the regolith in tropical areas often deep?

10 What are tafoni?

11 Make a labelled sketch of Figure 12 to show how the grooves and joints were weathered.

12 a Why has weathering made the rock in Figure 13 so pitted and 'lumpy'?
   b What will eventually happen to this rock?

31

The story of tors

Figure 14 *A tor*

Figure 15 *A distant view of tors*

Lone outcrops of solid rock are perched on the granite hilltops and ridges of Dartmoor. These are called **tors** (Figure 14). From a distance, tors look like piles of large boulders (Figure 15).

Tors could have been formed in several different ways.

Tors in the tropics

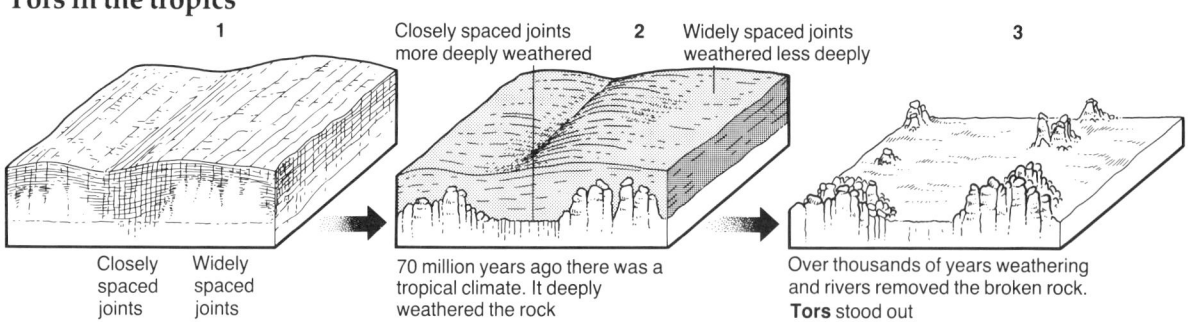

Figure 16 *How a tor was formed*

Some scientists think the Dartmoor tors were made by deep chemical weathering under a tropical climate 70 million years ago (Figure 16). Weathering was deeper where joints were closer together. Blocks of granite remained where joints were more widely spaced. In time, rivers stripped off the weathered rock above. The granite blocks were left on the higher land as tors.

Exercise

13 a Make a labelled sketch of Figure 14.
    b Explain how tropical weathering could have formed the tor.

Tors in the cold

Figure 17 *A millstone grit tor*

Figure 18 *Clitter*

Another idea is that tors were formed more recently by intense frost shattering during the Ice Age. Millstone grit tors in the Pennines may have been formed in this way (Figure 17).

The slopes near tors are littered with boulders called **clitter** (Figure 18). These boulders have been broken off the tors. They were moved when the ground thawed and soil crept downslope during warmer periods of the Ice Age (Figure 19).

Tors today

Tors were formed under different climates from now. Today, weathering continues to change their shape. Frost and pressure release are at work, though chemical weathering is more effective.

In granite, the feldspar minerals are most easily weathered. They change to a clay called kaolinite. The granite minerals then crumble apart leaving grains of coarse quartz sand called **growan**.

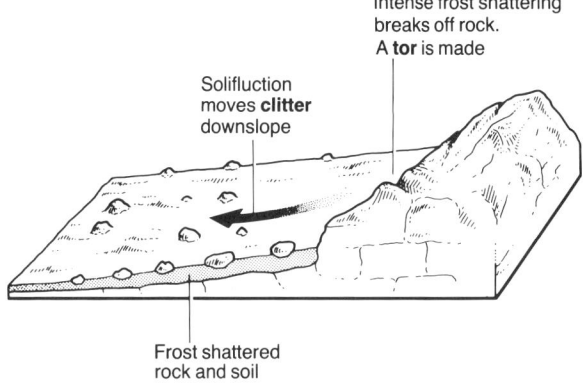

Figure 19 *How clitter was formed*

Exercises

14 Write down a heading 'Tors in the cold'. Sort these statements into their correct order:
a tor was formed ... clitter moved down the slope ... granite was frost shattered ... during a cold period of the Ice Age ... blocks of granite were broken off ... in warmer periods the ground thawed.

15 Name a piece of evidence to show that tors are still being weathered.

2.3 The sloping land

Walking or cycling up a steep slope is quite a struggle. Sledging down one is great fun. But we often do not notice how steep or gentle slopes are.

Making slopes

Slopes are first made when land is uplifted and rivers and seas cut into the land (Figure 1). Most slopes have then been altered by two processes.

Firstly the land surface is broken up by weathering. Next the soil and rock regolith flows, slides, falls or is washed away (Figure 2).

Figure 1 *A landscape of slopes*

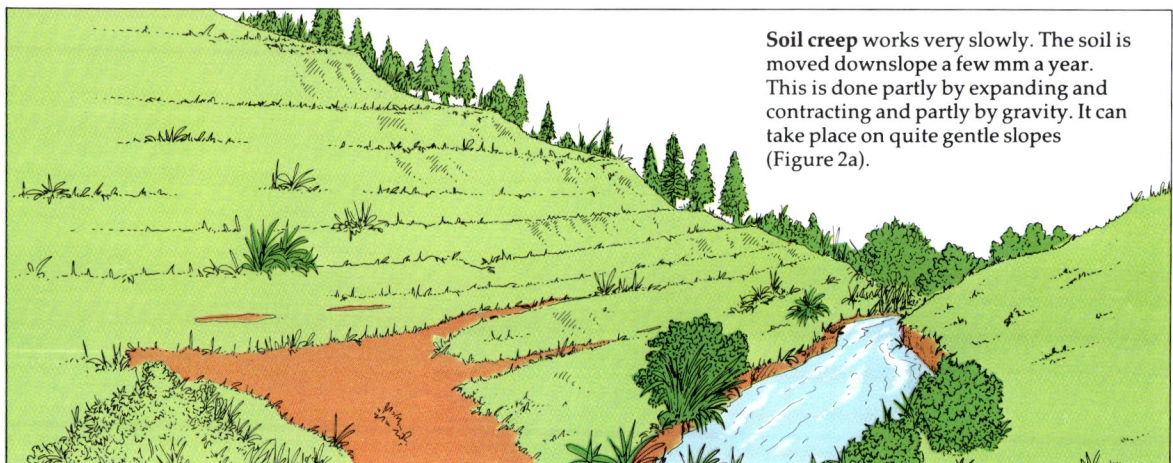

Soil creep works very slowly. The soil is moved downslope a few mm a year. This is done partly by expanding and contracting and partly by gravity. It can take place on quite gentle slopes (Figure 2a).

Figure 2a *Soil creep*

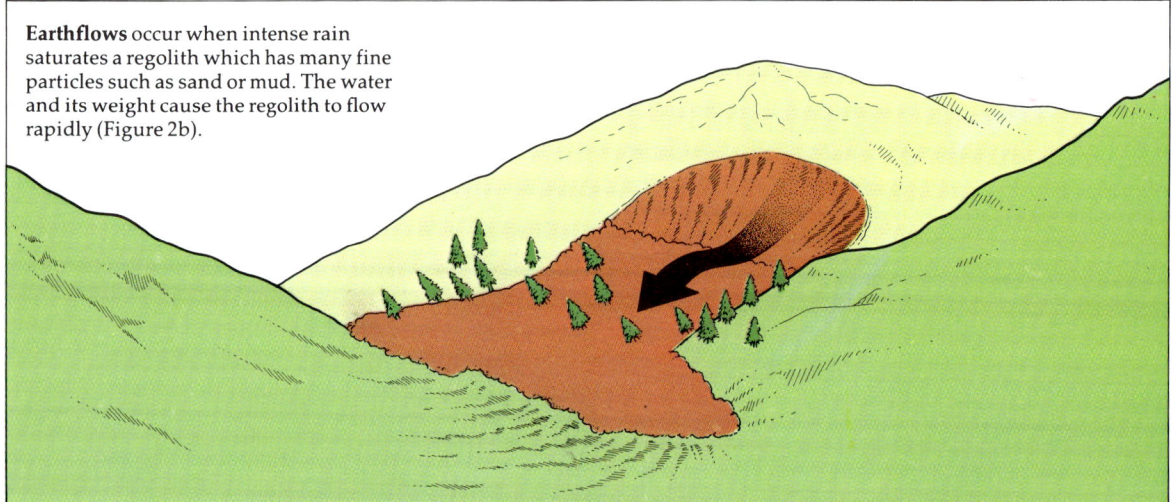

Earthflows occur when intense rain saturates a regolith which has many fine particles such as sand or mud. The water and its weight cause the regolith to flow rapidly (Figure 2b).

Figure 2b *Earthflow*

Landslides are more rapid still. They can be very large and include solid rock as well as the weathered layers. The rocks slip or slump down along a line of weakness. This can be a bedding plane or weak clays. Often the overlying rocks become saturated and heavier with water. Their weight wrenches them from the rock beneath (Figure 2c).

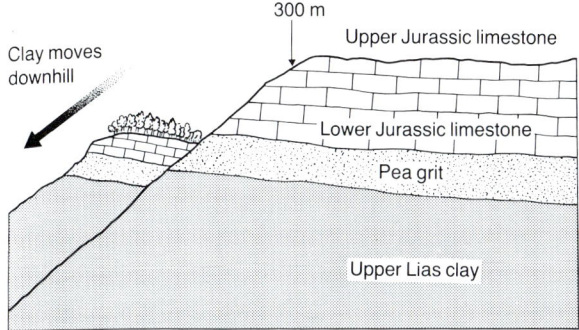

Figure 2c *Landslip*

Scree slopes build up below cliffs called **crags** and at the foot of mountainsides (Figure 2d). The larger, heavier boulders often roll to the bottom of the scree slope. Screes settle at an angle of around 35°. This is the **angle of repose**.

Figure 2d *Screes*

Heavy rain can saturate the ground. Water begins to flow over the surface as a thin sheet called **sheet flow**. Heavy raindrops hit the soil at a speed of about 7 m per second. They splash soil particles down the slope. It is estimated that 1.25 hours of heavy rainfall can move 225 tonnes of soil per hectare! Sheet flow and raindrop impact are forms of **surface wash** (Figure 2e).

Figure 2e *Surface wash*

Exercise

1 Match these words with the correct description:
   Words
   earthflow...soil creep...screes...landslides...surface wash.

   Descriptions
   slow movement of soil downslope...
   rocks and regolith slipping over the underlying rock...
   moving soil by raindrop splashes or a thin sheet of water...
   rocks which have fallen off crags...
   mud and soil flowing downslope after heavy rain.

Figure 3 *The retreat of limestone scarps in Salop*

Moving slopes

Slopes are continually being changed. Rock is weathered and then transported away so that the slope wears back and down. Surface wash causes slopes in lowland areas to wear back by up to a metre in a thousand years.

Wearing back

Slopes are changed in different ways. Where resistant rocks lie over weaker ones, the slope wears back keeping the same slope angle (Figure 3). This process is called the **parallel retreat of slopes**. In the UK, chalk and limestone escarpments wear back like this.

Many valley slopes wear down to a more gentle angle (Figure 4). This is called **slope decline**.

Exercises

2 a Make a sketch of the photo in Figure 3.
   b Draw and label it to show how the escarpment was worn back.

3 a Name the process making the valley slopes in Figure 4.
   b How is it different from the 'parallel retreat' process?

Figure 4 *Grindel Brook*

The effect of slopes

The angle at which the land slopes affects what people do. Flat or gently sloping land can cause drainage problems. However, houses, railways and airports are best built on such land. Steep slopes make building and the use of machinery difficult or impossible (Figure 5).

Slope angles are measured in degrees. Most slopes are less than 35°, except on mountains or cliffs along the coast.

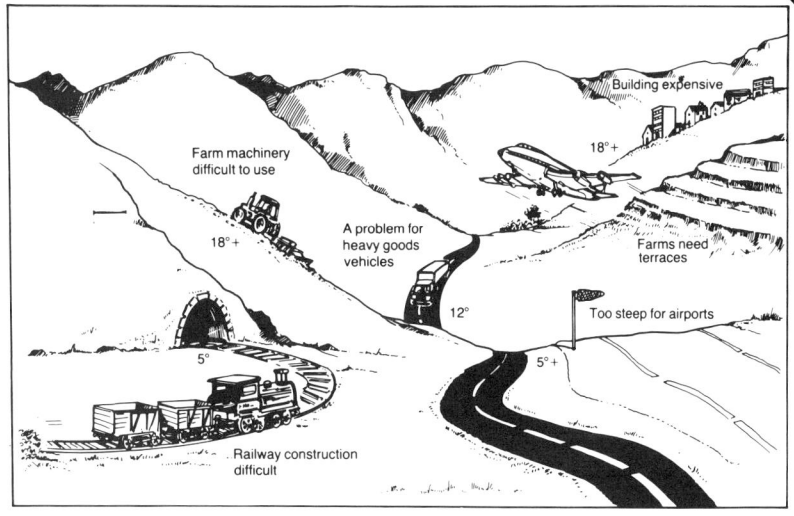

Figure 5 *How slopes affect land use*

Exercises

4 Study Figure 6.
   a Sketch and describe the ways different slopes are used.
   b Which land uses on Figure 5 would be difficult to have on Figure 6? Give reasons for your answer.

5 Make a sketch or a chart like this to show how slopes are used in your local area:

Type of slope eg steep etc . . .	Use of slope

Figure 6 *Using slopes, Rio de Janeiro*

Slopes on the move

Large areas of the city of Bath are built on slipped limestones, sands and clays. Roman and Medieval Bath was built on stable clay and alluvium rock. In the 18th century its famous Georgian crescents and terraces spread up the sides of the Avon Valley onto **landslips** (Figure 7). The weight of buildings caused new slips and damaged homes. It was to avoid these problems that Hedgemead Park was laid out on a landslip (Figure 8).

Most of the landslips are hundreds of years old. Even so, new building is done with care. The landslips are drained, surveyed and piles are used. This is expensive but safe.

Figure 7   *Bath*

Figure 8   *Hedgemead Park*

Slipping rocks

The geology and steep valley sides were the main causes of landslipping. Limestone overlies clay or sands. The clays and sands are weaker rocks which became well-lubricated after heavy rains. As a result they slipped downhill carrying the limestone with them. These rocks now form a rubble up to 40 m thick (Figure 9).

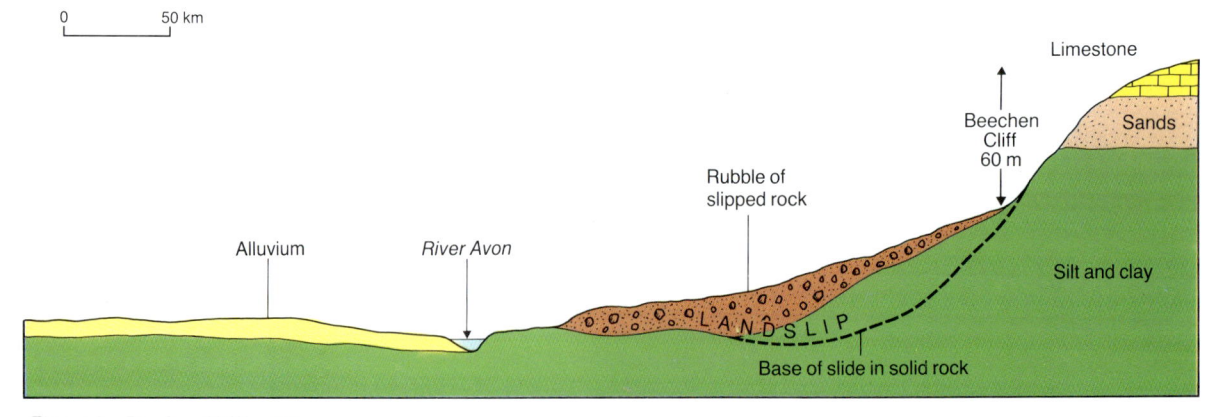

Figure 9   *Beechen Cliff landslip*

Cracks from cambering

At nearby Radstock, builders faced another geological problem. The surface layer of solid rock had become bent by slipping downhill (Figure 10). This bending caused the limestone and mudstone rock to split into cracks called **gulls** (Figure 11). The bending of rock strata in this way is called **cambering**.

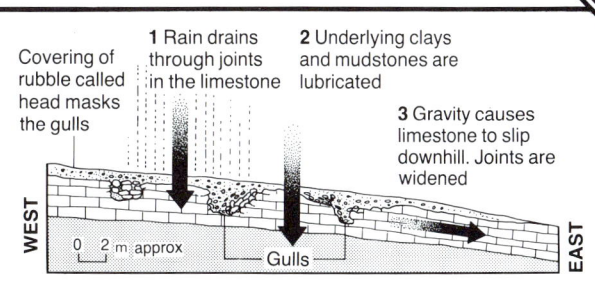

Figure 10 *Cambering*

Shifting homes

A housing estate was planned for this site. Once the gulls had been discovered the builder had to redesign the estate (Figure 12). The number of houses was cut from 92 to 78. Garages were built on concrete rafts and sited in places with most gulls. The foundations of the houses had to be strengthened. Gulls were filled with concrete plugs. Some were bridged by concrete beams which held up the house walls.

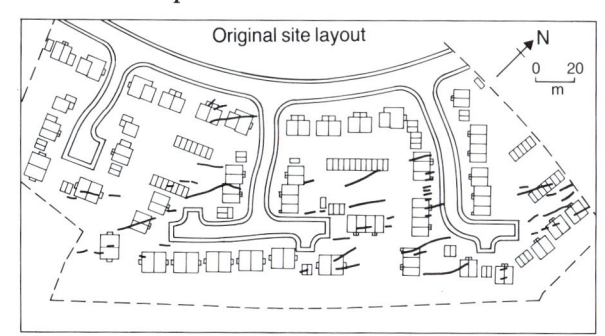

☐ Detached
▥ Semi-detached
▥ Garages
— Gulls

Figure 11 *A limestone gull*

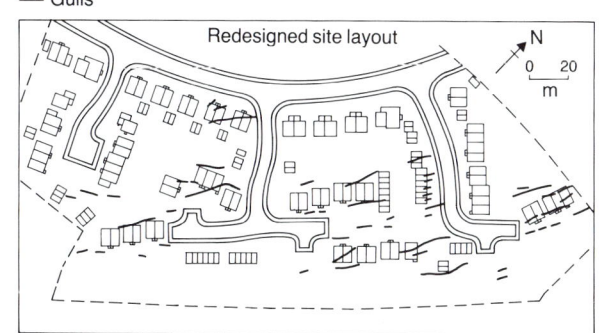

Figure 12 *Radstock housing plans*

Exercises

6 a Make a sketch of Figure 9.
   b Describe how such landslips have affected building in Bath.

7 a Describe how cambering changed the building of the Radstock housing estate. Mention:
      gulls ... number of houses ... garages ... plugs and beams.
   b Which of these changes can you see on Figure 12?

2.4 The wasting land

Soil is a precious layer. Yet nearly three billion tonnes of soil are swept from the USA each year. Two tonnes are lost from each hectare of farmland!

Making soils

Soils are made from weathered rock, rotting plants and living organisms, such as bacteria. Together, the rock minerals and living things give food for plants. Most of this is in the **topsoil** which farmers plough and sow (Figure 1).

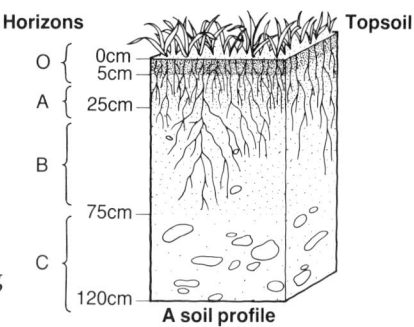

Figure 1 *A soil profile*

Wasting soils

Soils take thousands of years to form. But farming can cause the topsoil to be blown or washed away in a few years. This is called **soil erosion**. West Tennessee farms lose 67 million tonnes a year! Severe soil erosion has a big effect on farmers (Figures 2 and 3).

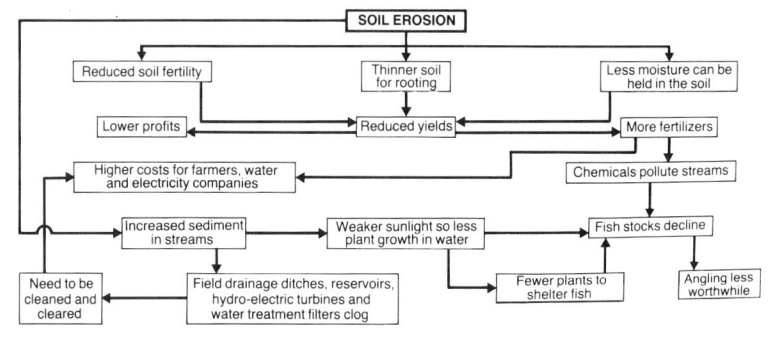

Figure 2 *The impact of soil erosion*

Planting in rows

The Tennessee farmers find that soya beans and corn are profitable crops and are good feedstuffs for their pigs and cattle. However, beans and corn are **row crops** which have plenty of bare soil between each plant (Figure 3a). Modern machinery needs larger fields so hedges have been dug up. It keeps land freer of weeds so it is easier to harvest. These changes leave the soil unprotected.

Sheet erosion

The heavy rainfall of 1250 mm per annum results in **sheet** and **rill erosion** (Figure 3b). Runoff water flows away as a thin sheet or in channels a few centimetres deep.

Figure 3a *Row crops*

Figure 3b *Sheet erosion*

SOS Save our soils

Farmers in Tennessee are trying several methods of **soil conservation**. Better crop and **land management** is raising yields and reducing soil erosion.

One method is the ploughing of slopes along the contours called **contour ploughing**. Alternate strips of different crops are planted and this is called **strip cropping** (Figure 4). These methods help stop soil being washed downslope.

Figure 4 *Strip cropping and contour ploughing*

Stalks and stubble

Another method of **soil conservation** is to keep the soil covered with plants. This is called **no-till cropping**. Stalks and stubble are left in the ground after the harvest to trap moisture for the next crop (Figure 5).

Heavy rain may flow away as a stream of water. Grass waterways help channel this away without becoming gullies.

Figure 5 *No-till cropping*

Gully erosion

On steeper slopes the runoff flows more rapidly. Grooves several metres deep are cut. This **gully erosion** makes it difficult to use farm machinery (Figure 3c).

Figure 3c *Gully erosion*

Exercises

1. a What is soil erosion?
   b How is it caused? Use words such as: farmers ... rainfall ... steep slopes (Figure 3).
   c Write down one fact to show that soil erosion in West Tennessee is a serious problem.

2. Study Figure 2.
   How does soil erosion affect the following people?
   Farmers ... Fishermen ... Hydro-electric engineers

3. Make labelled sketches of Figures 4 and 5 to show how farmers try to conserve their soil.

4. How do these figures show better 'land management'?

The spread of deserts

About 35 per cent of the Earth's land is turning to desert (Figure 6). Vegetation is being removed and bare soil exposed then eroded. Water supplies dry up and land near deserts is invaded by sand. These changes are called **desertification** (Figure 7).

These changes are putting at least 850 million people at risk. They cannot find water or grow food.

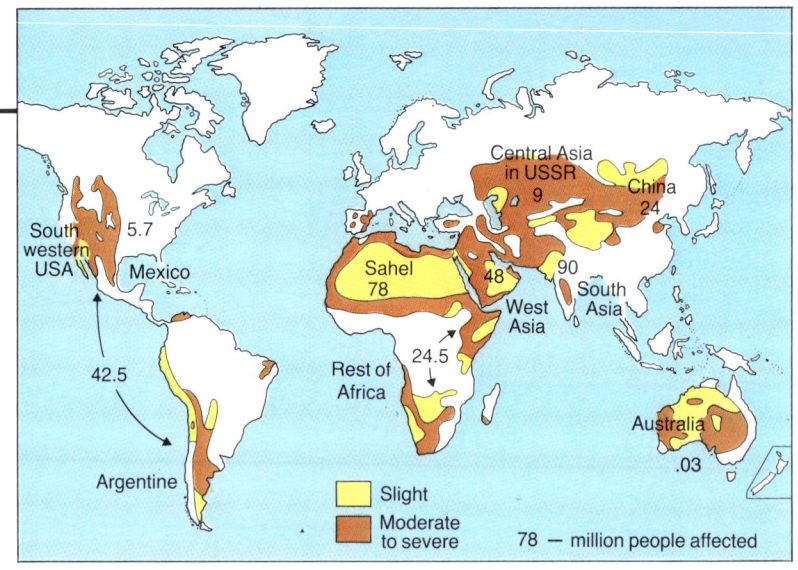

Figure 6 *Desertification throughout the world*

Figure 7a *Overgrazing around a waterhole*

Figure 7b *Salt from irrigation makes soil infertile*

Figure 7c *Mangrove forest destroyed for charcoal*

Suffering from deserts

Desertification is most widespread in developing countries where most people survive by farming. If crops fail and animals die, **famine** spreads and people die. Many leave their homes and lands in a desperate search for food and water (Figure 8).

Figure 8 *Refugees from drought*

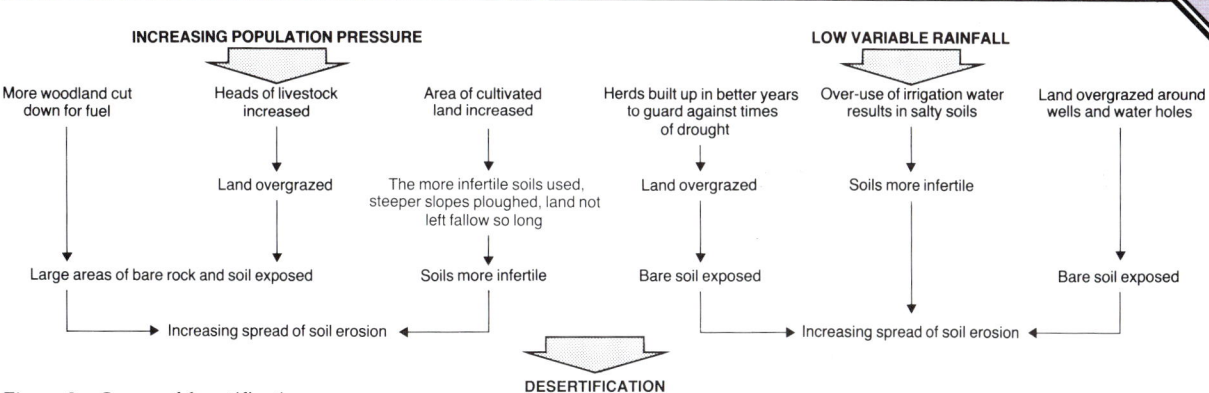

Figure 9 Causes of desertification

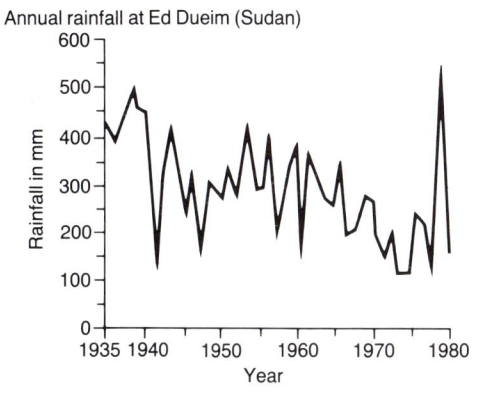

Figure 10 Rainfall in Sudan

Making deserts

Both people and nature play a part in desertification (Figure 9). **Semi-arid** areas such as the African Sahel, have unreliable rainfall and sometimes droughts (Figure 10). Land is **overgrazed** as farmers search for pasture for their animals. Cutting down trees and shrubs for fuelwood is another problem. This exposes more soil to erosion.

In some countries, the increasing population forces people to farm on steep slopes. Rain then washes the unprotected soil away.

Salty land

Too much salt can build up in soil where irrigation is poorly used (Figure 7). The effect is called **salination**. Over 30 per cent of irrigated land in Mexico is affected by salination.

Exercises

5   Use Figure 7 to describe desertification.

6   What is one result of desertification shown on Figure 8? Why does it happen?

7   List the areas and people suffering desertification (Figure 6). Put the areas with the most people first.

8   Which is the main cause of desertification? People, nature, or both?
    Use Figures 7, 9 and 10 to write an answer.

9   What is the connection between Figure 11 and desertification?

Figure 11 Fuelwood for cities

Figure 12 *Overgrazing around a well*

Figure 13 *A new well*

The Rendille people

The Rendille people of Northern Kenya are **nomadic pastoralists**. They have herds of cattle, sheep, goats and camels which provide them with milk, meat and clothing. There are about 150 000 animals in their herds.

The climate is **semi-arid**. People wander up to 350 km a year in search of water and pasture. The Rendille are a poor people. Few animals are sold and most of these for low prices.

Lives at risk

The people's way of life is now at risk. They sometimes lose one-third of their animals in a drought. The rangelands have been **overgrazed** because pasture is scarce. This exposes the land to erosion by wind and water (Figure 12).

IPAL

The letters IPAL stand for the **Integrated Project in Arid Lands**. This project seeks to improve all parts of the people's daily lives (Figure 13). The problems are closely linked so they all need to be tackled at the same time (Figure 14).

The problems	The IPAL Plan
Low, unreliable rainfall	26 new hand-dug wells, each serving a 15 km radius
95% of people illiterate	Improved education. Taught skills in farming
Land overgrazed	Controlled grazing. Rangelands used according to the quality of the pasture
Low prices for stock. Livestock sales infrequent. Animals have to be sold in poor condition	Better prices and easier marketing. More widespread veterinary service
Encourage people to save money gained by selling off surplus stock	Encourage people to use banks. Easier access for banks
40% of area not used because of raiding by other tribes	Improved policing. Tribes given title to lands
Low incomes. Only 10% of stock sold	More stock to be sold

Figure 14 *IPAL: the Integrated Project in Arid Lands*

Exercises

10 a Describe the way of life of the Rendille.
    b What do you think is the main problem in their lives?

11 Study Figure 14.
    How will IPAL tackle these problems?
    Mention: lack of security … lack of money … low rainfall … low prices for stock … illiteracy

12 IPAL is an integrated project.
    a What does this mean?
    b Why is it a sensible way to help the Rendille?

UNIT 3 Rivers and coasts

3.1 Introduction

Landscapes slowly change shape by natural processes over millions of years. People are changing all that. The natural processes are being disturbed by new technology, increasing demands for land and an increasing world population.

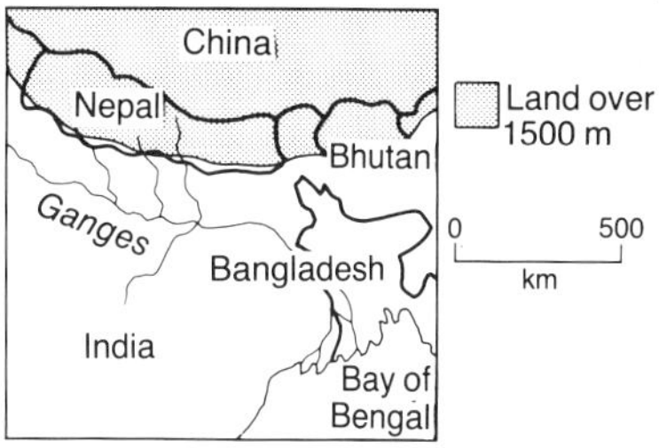

Figure 1 *Location of the Himalayas*

Agents for change

The Himalayas mountain range is being worn down by rain, ice and rivers (Figure 1). Soil and broken rock begins its journey to the sea in mountain streams. Bare slopes and deep valleys show how much material has already been removed (Figure 2).

Larger rivers such as the Ganges, carry the load to the sea. This process of removing rock and wearing down the landscape is called **erosion**. Ice and rivers are two of the **agents of erosion**.

Figure 2 *Bare hillsides in Nepal*

No time to adjust

People living in the mountains are playing an increasing part in speeding up the erosion. When trees are cut down for farmland, the soil loses its protection and is washed away by rain (Figure 3).

The result is felt in the lowlands. Swollen rivers choked by soil and rock debris burst their banks. Crops and homes are destroyed and lives are lost.

Figure 3 *Newspaper extract about soil erosion*

EROSION SWEEPS HIMALAYAN MOUNTAINS DOWN TO THE SEA

The Himalayas are disappearing into the sea. Tons of soil are being stripped from every acre of the mountains by each monsoon, destroying the land on which Nepal's people depend. In the worst areas, 80 tons are ripped from each acre. Villagers watch all night for landslides during the monsoons. Little wonder — 20 000 landslides have been recorded in a single day.
In the three decades since Everest was conquered, half of the forests that once coated Nepal's mountains have been cut down and the rest are expected to dissapear by the end of the century.
The plains are dangerous too. The mountain soil covers the river-beds, raising them 6 to 12 inches a year. Inevitably the rivers flood and the land on their banks is swept away. The soil is swept down the Ganges river system and is forming a new island in the Bay of Bengal.

A new dilemma

The answer seems simple. Trees should not be cut down and replanting must take place. This is hard to do in a country where an increasing number of people must grow food to survive.

Exercises

1 a Explain the term 'agents of erosion'.
   b Study Figure 2. How can you tell that the Himalayas mountains are being eroded?
   c How is the soil and broken rock removed from the mountains?
   d Where does the eroded material end up?

2 a Explain why the amount of erosion is increasing in the Himalayas.
   b In what ways could a river change to cope with more material? (Hint: shape and size.)
   c What happens when the river cannot adjust in time?
   d Why is it so difficult to solve the problem?

3.2 Rivers at work

Rivers are nature's conveyor belts and sculptors. They take away soil and rock. They wear away old landforms and make new ones.

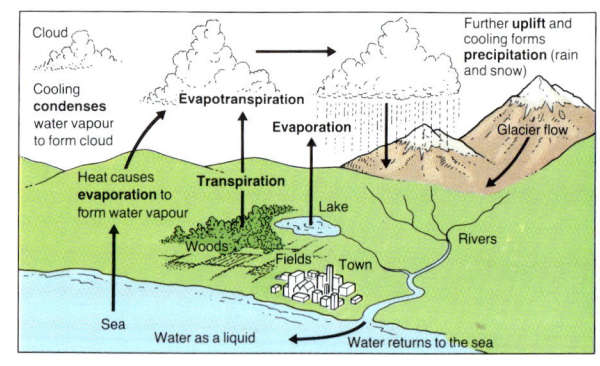

Figure 1 *The water cycle*

Round and round

The oceans give an endless supply of water for streams and rivers (Figure 1). The sun's heat evaporates water, changing it to **water vapour**. This falls to Earth again as rain or snow. Rivers complete the link by returning water to the oceans. This link is called the **water cycle**.

Getting through

Water takes many routes on its way to the rivers (Figure 2). Some enters as **run-off** by flowing down valley slopes.

A large amount sinks into the soil and moves down into the rock below. More water sinks through a permeable rock such as limestone, than through an impermeable rock such as granite. It fills up spaces until the rock is saturated.

The water table

The **water table** is the level of water in the rocks. Water held back in the rock is said to be in **storage**. Some water from the rocks later comes out as **springs**.

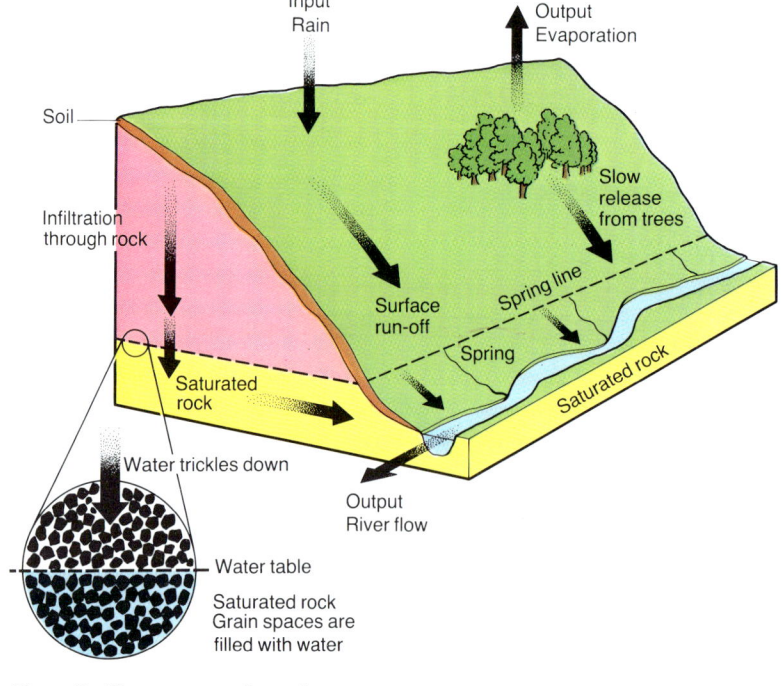

Figure 2 *How water reaches a river*

Exercises

1 Draw some boxes linked by arrows to show the water cycle. Label each box.

2 Write a definition for each of these terms:
   run-off
   saturated

3 a Why is storage greater in a rock such as limestone than in one such as granite?
   b Draw a sketch to show why and where springs occur.
   c Why does the level of the water table change during the year?

Taking its time

Rain flows into a river as run-off within a few hours. The amount of water flowing in a river is called the **discharge**. A **hydrograph** shows what happens (Figure 3).

The river rises soon after the rain, but it keeps flowing long after the rain has stopped. Water is only slowly released from vegetation, soil and rock. It may take days, weeks and even years before the water enters the river.

Changes in discharge

A river's discharge changes from day to day and from month to month as the weather changes. This changing pattern of flow over the year is called the river's **regime** (Figures 4 and 5).

Annual average rainfall for the Amazon Basin (mm)
J   F   M   A   M   J   J   A   S   O   N   D
277 251 318 286 221 94 52 46 64 111 163 217

Figure 5 *Rainfall in the Amazon Basin*

A water budget

A **water budget** shows how much water goes to different places (Figure 6). This information can be used to predict if there might be a **flood** when the river bursts its banks.

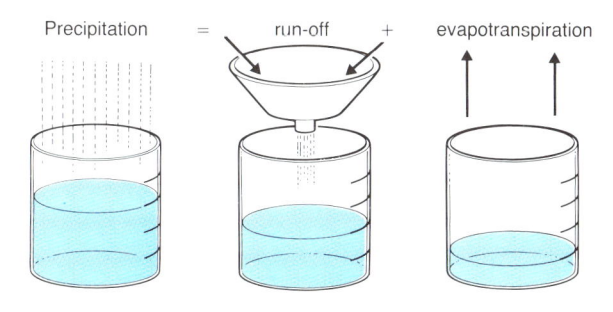

Precipitation = run-off + evapotranspiration

Figure 6 *The water budget*

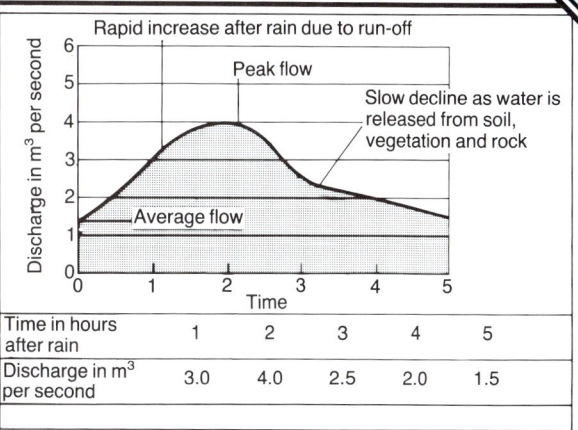

Figure 3 *A storm hydrograph*

Rapid increase after rain due to run-off
Peak flow
Slow decline as water is released from soil, vegetation and rock
Average flow

Time in hours after rain	1	2	3	4	5
Discharge in m³ per second	3.0	4.0	2.5	2.0	1.5

River Amazon discharge at Obidos (1975)

	J	F	M	A	M	J	J	A	S	O	N	D
Discharge in m³/s (cubic metres per second)	128	160	190	221	241	246	233	211	177	129	89	88

Obidos is 200 km from the mouth of the Amazon

Figure 4 *River Amazon regime*

Exercises

4 Invent two hydrographs to show:
   a very rapid run-off in a desert area where there is no vegetation to hold back water
   b an area of dense woodland and permeable rock where most water is held in storage.

5 a Draw graphs to show both the river discharge and the rainfall at Manaus.
   b How closely is rainfall linked to discharge? Explain your answer.

6 How can each of these things affect the water budget? Explain your answer with examples, e.g. what might be the effect of high or low temperatures?
   Precipitation
   The temperature
   The amount of vegetation
   The soil and rock type

Channel shape

Water flows in a stream or river **channel** (Figure 7). A **cross-section** shows the shape of the channel. Depth measurements are needed to find the **area** of the river's cross-section.

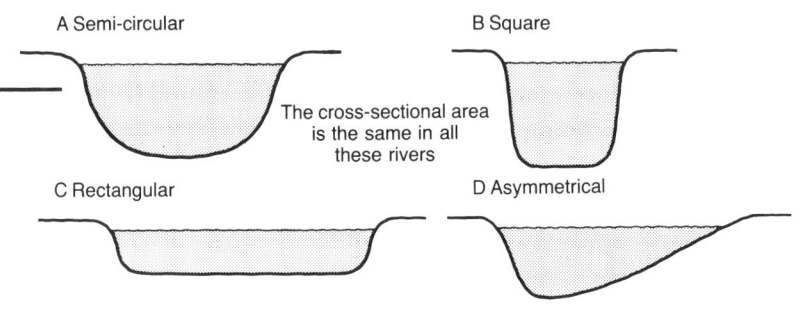

A Semi-circular
B Square
C Rectangular
D Asymmetrical

The cross-sectional area is the same in all these rivers

Figure 7 *Channel cross-sections and areas*

Getting your feet wet

Measuring a river's discharge means getting wet feet. Taking river measurements is a matter of teamwork (Figure 8).

River energy

A flowing river has **energy**. The amount of energy depends on **velocity** (speed) of the discharge. A steep slope gives a greater speed and more energy than a gentle slope.

Discharge = cross-sectional area × velocity

Metre ruler or pole
Tape
Stop watch
Float
Clip board and record sheet
A computer can help with the calculation
Take several velocity readings from different points across the river. Work out an average
Slower flow
Faster flow
Slower flow
Cross-sectional area
Wetted perimeter
Velocity can also be measured with a flow meter

Figure 8 *Measuring a stream*

Causing friction

Energy is used up as the river rubs against the bed and sides causing **friction**. The bed and sides of a channel add up to a cross-section measurement called the **wetted perimeter**. A semi-circle channel shape has the lowest wetted perimeter so there is least friction. The fastest flow is in the middle of the channel where friction is least.

Rocky beds

A rocky bed makes the river bubble and look full of energy. In fact, the rocks cause extra friction so there is less energy for erosion (Figure 9).

Figure 9 *A mountain stream*

Exercises

7   a Draw four different river cross-sections on a sheet of graph paper. Try to make each cover the same number of squares.
    b Use Figure 8 to describe how to organize measuring in a local stream. Mention:
       number of people and jobs each does
       equipment
       method of survey and any problems

8   Describe how the river in Figure 9 is using most of its energy. Use these words:
    friction ... energy ... cross-section ... velocity.

Energy for erosion

Rivers usually have enough energy left for some erosion (Figure 10). The force of flowing water breaks pieces off the banks. This force is called **hydraulic action**.

The pieces rub against the sides and cause more erosion. This rubbing action is called **abrasion**. Stones caught up in hollows swirl around to form potholes.

Solution is another way rivers erode. This happens when minerals in some rocks are dissolved by weak acids in the water then washed away.

Figure 10 *River erosion*

Moving the load

Material carried in a river is called its **load**. The load is carried by bumping along the bed, floating in suspension, or dissolved as a solution (Figure 11). This work is called **transportation**.

As the load is moved, the pieces rub against each other and the channel sides. This makes them smaller and more rounded. This process is called **attrition**.

Average suspended sediment load in kg per m^3

Yellow (China)	Ganges (India)	Amazon (Brazil)	Colorado (USA)
37·6	3·9	·1	27·5
1600	1451	400	135

Annual load in million tonnes

Figure 11 *Load carried in suspension*

Figure 12 *Transport and deposition*

Dropping the load

When a river slows down, some energy is lost and part of the load is dropped. This process is called **deposition** (Figure 12).

The larger stones are dropped first. Fine mud is carried further, then dropped to form a valley soil called **alluvium**. Some is dropped in a lake or the sea as a **delta**. (See Unit 3.4 p 63).

Exercises

9 Copy and complete these sentences.
   a Erosion caused by a river's velocity and weight is called ...
   b Acids in water cause ...
   c Potholes are made by ...

10 Study Figure 12.
   a Describe the size and shape of the load in the river bed.
   b Where might the load have come from?
   c What will happen to the stones in time?

Creeping slopes

Weathering breaks up rock on the valley slopes. Rain and gravity make soil and broken rock creep downslope (Figure 13). This exposes more rock to weathering and erosion. Rivers eventually carry the material away.

Cutting down

There is **vertical erosion** in upland areas as rivers cut out V-shaped valleys (Figure 14). The landscape is said to be **dissected**.

There are waterfalls or rapids where a hard band of rock resists erosion (Figure 15). Even these are worn back and down in time.

Figure 14 *A dissected upland in Algeria*

Figure 15 *Hardrow Force, Yorkshire Dales*

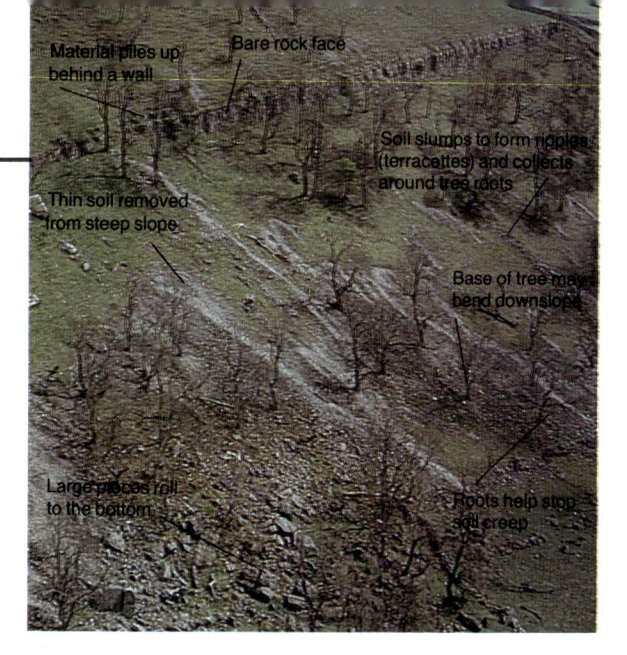

Figure 13 *Erosion on valley slopes*

Riffles and pools

The bed of a river is usually divided into deep sections called **pools**, then shallow sections called **riffles**. Energy builds up in the pools, then is used for downward erosion over the shallow and faster flowing riffles.

Exercises

11 Study Figure 13.
   a How is rock broken from a bare rock face?
   b Why is erosion faster from a slope with no soil or vegetation?
   c Why do mounds of soil pile up near the base of the trees?
   d How is rock and soil removed from the valley bottom?

12 a Draw a sketch of Figure 14. Add labels to show where material has been removed by rivers.
    b How do you think this landscape will change in the future?

13 a How do riffles and pools affect a river's speed of flow?
    b Why is vertical erosion more active over a riffle than a pool?

Side to side

Rivers seldom flow straight. They wind in a series of bends called **meanders**. Water flows faster on the outside of a meander bend. This causes erosion (Figure 16). There is deposition on the slower flowing inside bend. The whole meander snakes downstream.

Sometimes the river breaks through the **neck** of a meander. An **ox-bow** lake is left where the river used to flow. These lakes soon become overgrown and filled in with alluvium.

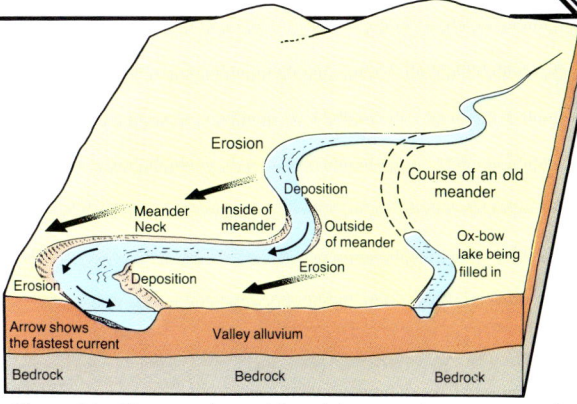

Figure 16 *River erosion and deposition*

Building a flood plain

Meandering causes sideways (**lateral**) erosion in the valley bottom. **Spurs** are worn back. This widens the valley and gives a flat **flood plain** (Figure 17).

In flood time, water spills up over the banks onto the flood plain carrying a fine mud called **silt**. This is soon dropped as the water spreads out over the flood plain. In this way, rivers build up their valley floors. Some flow over a thick bed of silt without cutting into the rock below.

A natural levee

As floodwater drains back into the river, silt and coarser material is left on the banks. This can build up to form **levees** (Figure 18).

Some large rivers such as the Mississippi, flow at a level higher than their flood plain. The only protection against flooding is the levee.

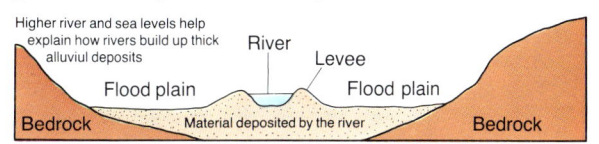

Figure 18 *A natural levee*

Figure 17 *A river flood plain*

Exercises

14 a Draw a map to show a section of meandering river. Label in:
 where there is erosion and deposition
 deep and shallow places
  b Explain how a meander can snake downstream.
  c How do ox-bow lakes show past meandering?

15 Make a sketch of Figure 17. Add labels to name the features shown and how the river is changing the valley shape.

16 What materials would you expect to find in the bottom of a broad river valley? Explain how these materials got there.

Drainage basins

Tributary streams join the main river to form a **river system**. The area drained by a river system is called a **drainage basin** or **catchment area** (Figure 19).

When rain falls, it flows into one drainage basin. The higher land separating drainage basins is called a **watershed**. This can be a steep mountain ridge or a low hill with gentle slopes.

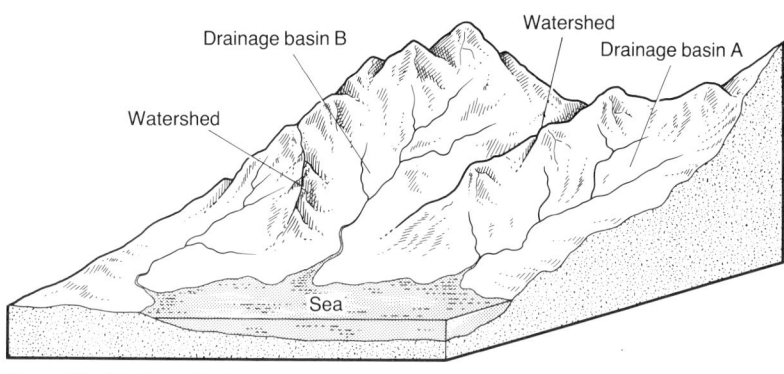

Figure 19 *Drainage basins*

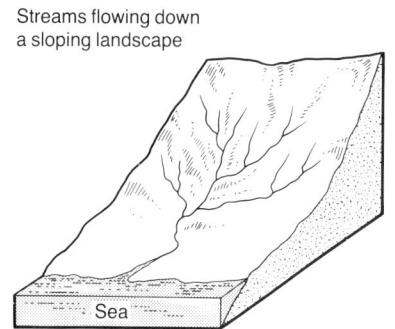

Figure 20 *Dendritic drainage*

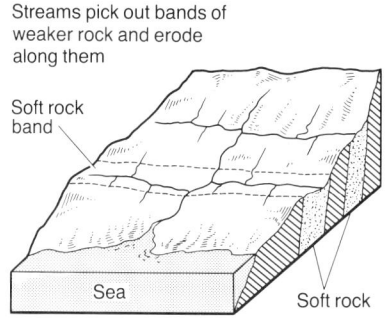

Figure 21 *Trellis drainage*

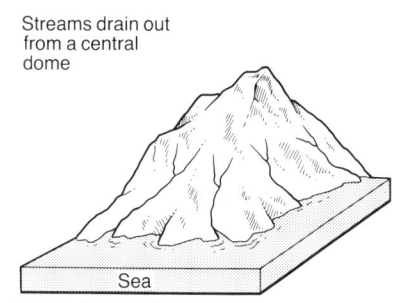

Figure 22 *Radial drainage*

Forming patterns

A river system makes a pattern of shapes. A **dendritic** pattern is shaped like tree branches (Figure 20). This usually forms on a landscape where rocks are the same, or where land is raised above sea level for the first time.

A **trellis** system is where streams join at right angles (Figure 21). Faults or bands of different rocks give lines of weakness which streams pick out.

In a **radial** pattern, streams flow out in all directions from a central dome (Figure 22).

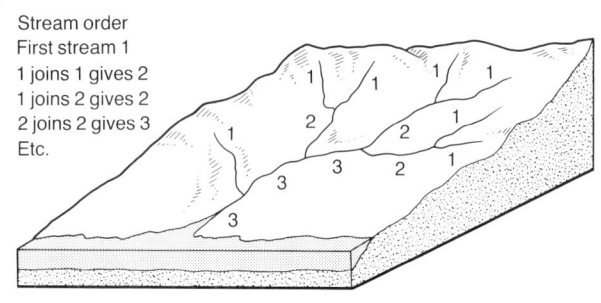

Stream order
First stream 1
1 joins 1 gives 2
1 joins 2 gives 2
2 joins 2 gives 3
Etc.

Figure 23 *Stream order*

All in order

Each stream in a river system can be given a number or **order** (Figure 23). This method of numbering helps describe a river's size and the number of tributaries in the system.

Exercises

17 a Draw a map to show the rivers in drainage basin B in Figure 19.
    b Number the rivers to show stream order.

18 Draw the three diagrams showing different drainage patterns (Figures 20, 21, 22). Add notes to explain why the patterns are different.

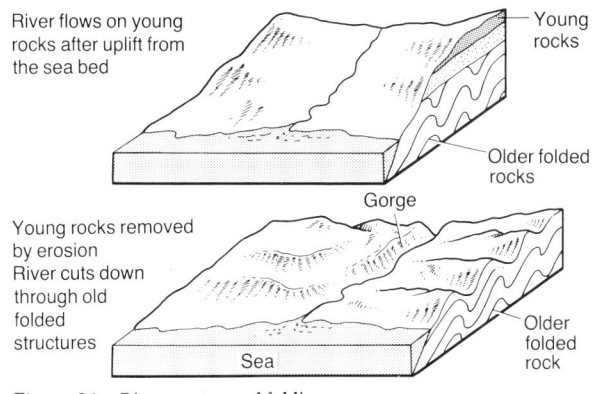

Figure 24 *River routes and folding*

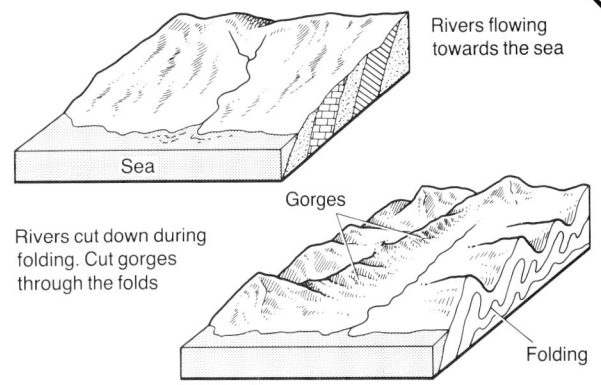

Figure 25 *River routes on an old structure*

Odd routes

Some rivers flow through hill ranges instead of around them, often through a steep **gorge**.

This can happen where the river is older than the hills. As the structure was folded up, the river kept pace by cutting down (Figure 24).

Sometimes, a river begins to flow on rocks laid down above a folded structure. Erosion removes the top layer but the river keeps cutting down on the same course (Figure 25).

The past uncovered

In south east England, rivers began to flow north and south down the slopes of an anticline about 30 million years ago. The centre of the anticline has been eroded, but the rivers follow their original course.

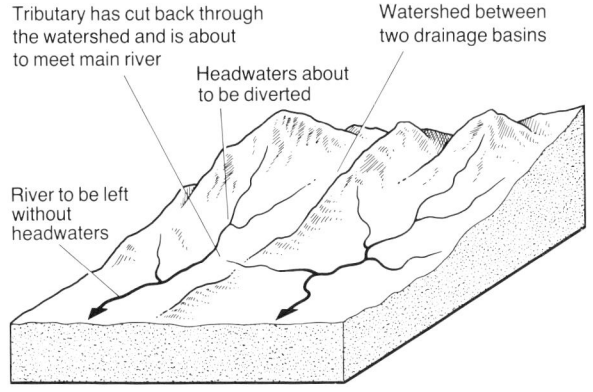

Figure 26 *River capture*

Taking over

River headwaters erode backwards. This moves the watershed back into the drainage basin next to it (Figure 26). As one drainage basin gets larger, rivers can be diverted from basin to basin in a process called **river capture**.

An empty valley is left called a **wind gap**. A sharp bend called an **elbow of capture** may show where the capture took place.

Exercises

19 a Use an atlas to draw a sketch map to show the course of the river Medway in south east England. Shade and name the hills and lowland it passes through.
    b Describe what is unusual about its route and why it flows in this direction.

20 a Draw a sketch map of the Columbia and Snake Rivers in the Rocky Mountains.
    b The mountain fold lines are mainly north to south. Describe what is unusual about the course taken by the rivers.
    c How could you explain their courses?

21 What evidence would you look for to see if river capture had taken place?

3.3 Rivers: the human impact

Few people live far from a river. In the past, whole civilizations depended on them. Today, they still play a part in people's ways of life.

Rivers and land use

Towns and villages were built at bridging points and near rivers for defence and for water supply. The rivers powered waterwheels for grinding flour and for industry. Today, water power drives turbines for electricity and river water is needed for cooling in industry.

Rivers are natural routes for moving goods (Figure 1). Valleys are routeways for roads and railways. The rich alluvial soils give fertile farmland. Many types of recreation now take place on and by rivers.

Figure 1 *Rivers as routes*

Unnatural rivers

Rivers are changed when they are used (Figure 2). Locks and weirs control a river's depth and speed. Diversion schemes can change their course and even take water from one drainage basin to another. Dams stop the normal changes in flow during the year and stop flooding.

All these things affect the river's normal work of erosion, transportation and deposition.

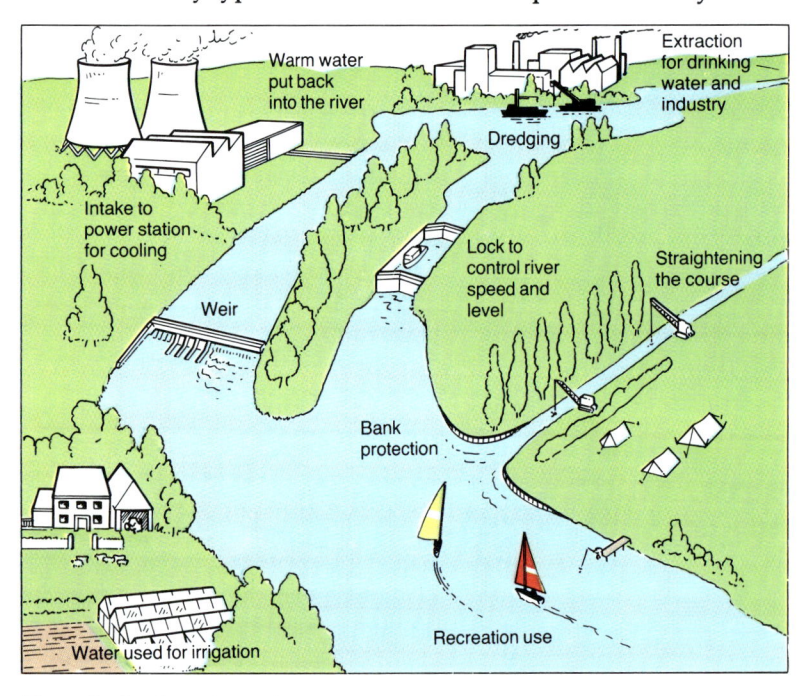

Figure 2 *Land use along a river*

Exercises

1. Draw a map of a real or imaginary river from its source in the mountains to where it enters the sea.
   Mark in the different ways the river is used along its course, for example: towns, transport, industry, reservoirs and recreation.

2. Study Figure 2. How do you think each of these things might be affected by how the river is being used?
   a Velocity
   b Discharge
   c Course
   d Depth and width

Figure 3 The Canon's Brook catchment area in Harlow

Land use change and drainage

Land use affects how quickly water reaches the rivers. In Harlow New Town, houses, factories and roads were built on farmland (Figures 3, 4 and 5). This increased the average flow in one stream by 30 per cent (Figure 6).

Rainwater ran into the new drains and flowed straight into the stream. There was less soil and vegetation to absorb the rainwater.

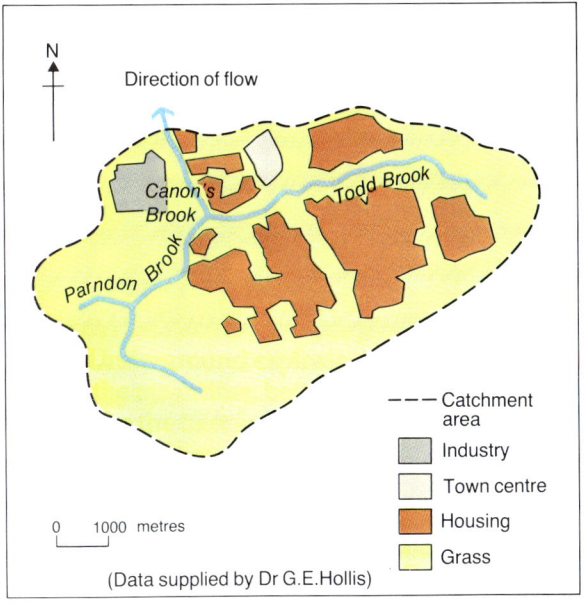

Figure 4 Canon's Brook catchment land use
(Data supplied by Dr G.E.Hollis)

- - - - Catchment area
Industry
Town centre
Housing
Grass

Land use change in the catchment area of the Canon's Brook, Harlow

	Percentage of rural land	
	before building	after building
Grass and soil	34	38
Woods and hedges	12	13
Arable farmland	64	34
Houses, paths, roads	0	15

Total catchment area 21 km²

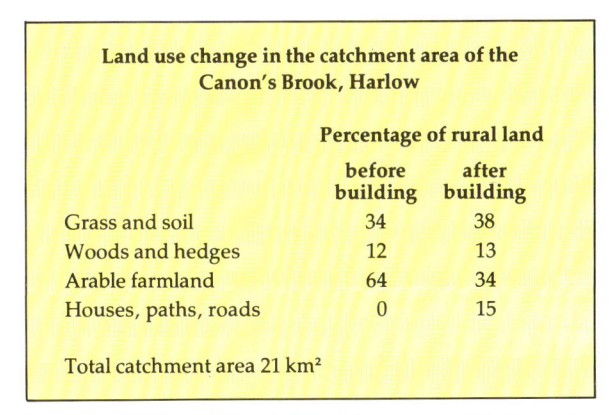

Figure 5 Land use change in the catchment area of the Canon's Brook, Harlow

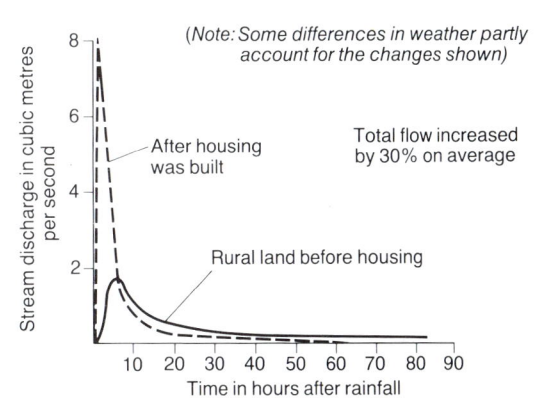

Figure 6 The Canon's Brook hydrograph

(Note: Some differences in weather partly account for the changes shown)

Total flow increased by 30% on average

After housing was built

Rural land before housing

Exercises

3 a Draw two bar graphs to illustrate the figures shown in Figure 5.
   b Use figures to describe how the natural ground surface was changed.
   c Describe the kind of building which has taken place in the area shown on Figure 3.

4 a Give reasons why rainwater runs into streams more rapidly from a built up area than from farmland.
   b Use figures from the hydrograph (Figure 6) to show how the stream's pattern of flow has been changed.

People at risk

The river valleys in Asia are some of the most fertile and densely settled rural areas in the world (Figure 7). **Floods** leave new soil on the fields.

Unexpected flooding brings death and destruction. The rising population and the need to grow even more food makes flood control even more urgent.

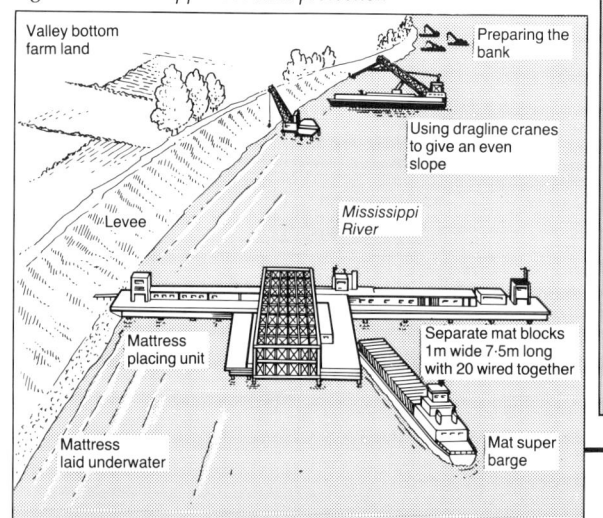

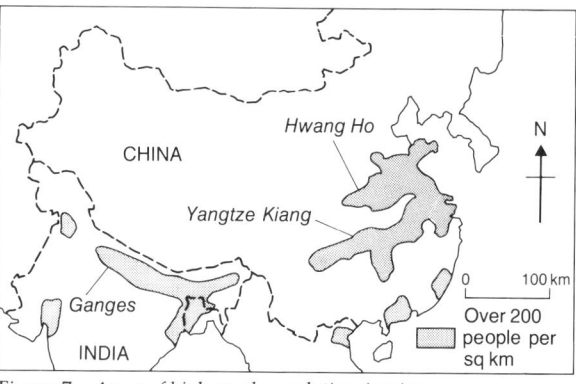

Figure 7 *Areas of high rural population density*

Bank protection

Chinese farmers have been trying to control flooding for 4000 years. The Yellow River is up to 10 metres higher than its valley bottom. Natural levees keep the water in. These levees have to be built up for extra protection. Even smaller rivers need bank protection (Figure 8).

Along the Mississippi in the USA, concrete walls called **revetments** help stop erosion (Figure 9). Stone-filled wire cages called **gabions** are a common method of bank protection in the UK.

Figure 8 *Repairing river banks in China*

Building dams

Flooding in lowlands can be controlled by building **dams** across narrow mountain streams. This stops the rapid increase in discharge after heavy rainfall. A dam across a broad lowland valley must be much wider. An extra problem is that people's homes and good farmland may be covered by a lake.

Figure 9 *Mississippi river bank protection*

Exercises

5 a Use an atlas to describe the population density along these major rivers in Asia:
      the Ganges in India
      Hwang Ho (Yellow River) in China
   b Find a rainfall map or graph of a monsoon area in Asia. How does this help explain why there is a high risk of flooding?
   c Why do people live near these rivers?

6 a What does Figure 8 tell you about flood control in a poor country? Mention:
      the method being used
      the technology available
      the need for flood control
   b How is the same job being done along the banks of the Mississippi? Explain why.
   c What do you think are the advantages and disadvantages of both mountain dams and lowland barrages in stopping flooding?

Let it flow

Floodwater which cannot be held back or kept in, may have to be diverted (Figure 10). Peak floodwater is taken out along a **floodway** to where no damage will be done.

Land management

Management of land use has reduced flooding in the Tennessee valley. Planting trees (**afforestation**) is one way to do this. Water is held back and peak run-off is reduced. Soil which can choke a river is kept on the land. Farming methods such as **contour ploughing** also reduce soil erosion (Figure 11).

Figure 10   *Diverting Mississippi floodwater*

Figure 11   *Crops being harvested along the contours*

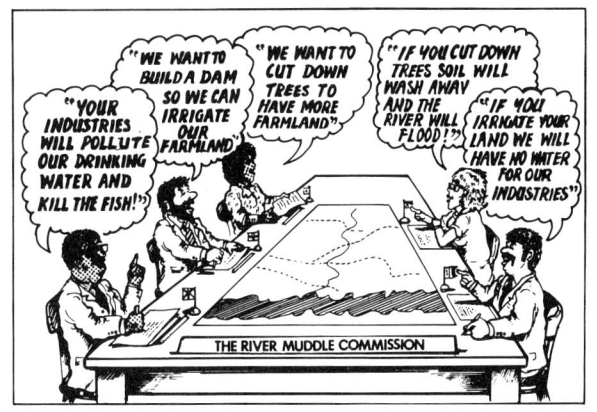

Figure 12   *Conflict over rivers*

Politics and flood control

Flood control is made more difficult when a river flows through more than one country (Figure 12). Soil erosion in one country becomes the cause of flooding in another. Agreement between governments does not come easily, especially when money is involved.

Taking a risk

In some places, the risk of flooding is low. Spending on flood control is not worth the cost. Allowing the land to flood in one place may even save greater problems further downstream.

Exercises

7   Study Figure 10.
    a   Why does the land need to be protected against flooding?
    b   Describe what has been done to contain the floodwater.

8   a   How can afforestation help stop flooding?
    b   Explain the term 'contour ploughing'.
    c   How can contour ploughing reduce soil erosion?

9   What is the problem illustrated in Figure 12?

The water industry

In England and Wales, rivers are managed by 10 **Water Authorities** (Figure 13). Each looks after one or more drainage basins. About 70 000 people work for these Authorities and in other branches of the water supply industry.

Water Authorities

Publicly owned Water Authorities are responsible for how water is used (Figure 14). Some politicians believe that Water Authorities should be run as private companies. Many people think this would mean dearer water and a poorer service.

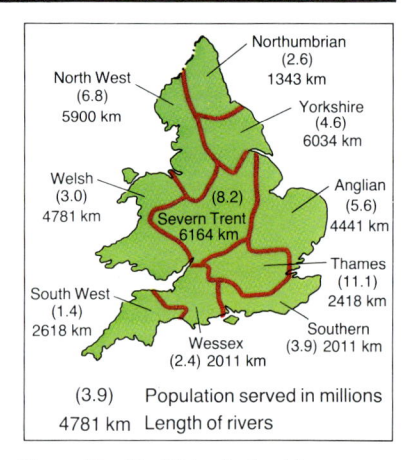

Figure 13 *The Water Authorities*

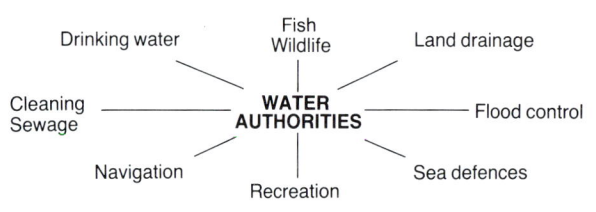

Northumbrian (2.6) 1343 km
North West (6.8) 5900 km
Yorkshire (4.6) 6034 km
Welsh (3.0) 4781 km
Severn Trent (8.2) 6164 km
Anglian (5.6) 4441 km
Thames (11.1) 2418 km
South West (1.4) 2618 km
Wessex (2.4) 2011 km
Southern (3.9) 2011 km

(3.9) Population served in millions
4781 km Length of rivers

Figure 14 *Responsibilities of Water Authorities*

WATER AUTHORITIES: Drinking water, Fish Wildlife, Land drainage, Cleaning Sewage, Flood control, Navigation, Recreation, Sea defences

Surface water abstraction England and Wales 1983	% of total abstraction
Water supply (homes)	45
Industry	15
Spray irrigation and agriculture (less than 1)	
CEGB (electricity)	36
Fish farming and watercress	4
(Other water supplies come from groundwater held in rocks)	

Figure 15 *Use of river water in England and Wales*

Exercises

10 a In which Water Authority area do you live?
    b Which river system has the largest drainage basin in the area?

11 a Use Figure 15 to draw a bar graph of different ways water is used.
    b Why is pollution control so important?

12 Choose any other country in Europe. Give yourself the job of dividing it up into Water Authority areas.
    a Draw or trace the rivers.
    b Draw a line around your areas.
    c Give each area a name.
    d See where the major cities are. Would you need to transfer water from one area to another? Draw how this might be done.
    e Would your Water Authorities be publicly owned or run by private companies?

Moving water

Water is taken out of rivers for farms and industry (Figure 15). This is called **abstraction**. There are fines for causing pollution and abstraction without permission. Water needs to be kept clean as 67 per cent of UK water supplies come from the rivers.

Water is moved between drainage basins by **water transfer** schemes to help out areas with a water shortage. In one scheme, water from the Elan Valley reservoir in Wales is piped to Birmingham in the West Midlands.

Limits to control

The Water Authorities do not control how land is used in the drainage basin. This makes the work of flood control more difficult.

The Yorkshire Derwent

The River Derwent flows through the mainly rural landscape of east Yorkshire (Figures 16, 17, 18, 19, 20). The Yorkshire Water Authority has to make sure that best use is made of the river, and that it is not spoilt by the different demands on it.

River Derwent statistics

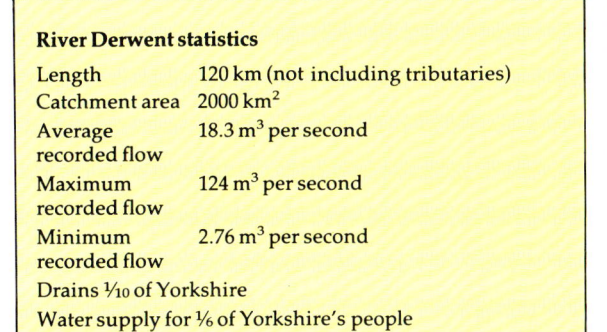

Length	120 km (not including tributaries)
Catchment area	2000 km^2
Average recorded flow	18.3 m^3 per second
Maximum recorded flow	124 m^3 per second
Minimum recorded flow	2.76 m^3 per second

Drains 1/10 of Yorkshire
Water supply for 1/6 of Yorkshire's people

Figure 16 *The Derwent statistics*

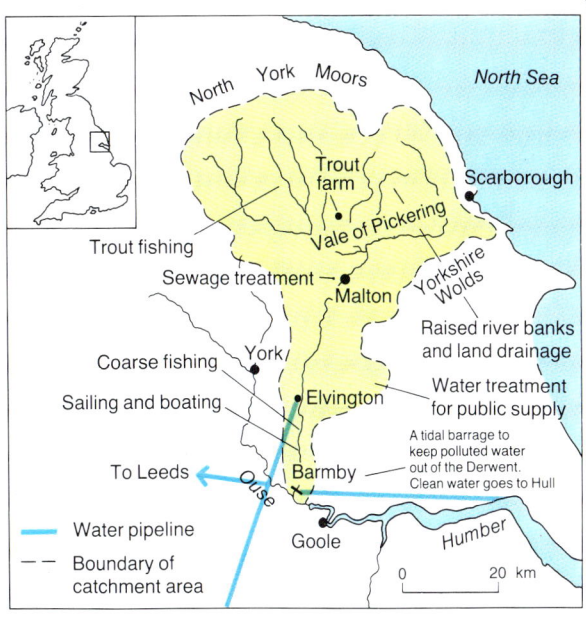

Figure 17 *The Yorkshire Derwent catchment area*

Figure 18 *Barmby sluice gates to stop tidal water flowing up the Derwent*

Figure 19 *The River Derwent source*

Figure 20 *Forge Valley*

Exercises

13 Draw a large map to show the River Derwent and its tributary streams. Label in these things:
- names of upland and lowland areas
- statistics for the catchment area
- a graph of discharge during the year

14 Use the map, figures and photographs to write a description of how the Derwent is used for:
- farming and fishing
- water supply
- navigation

3.4 The changing coast

The sea is one of nature's most powerful and relentless forces. This is why coastlines change faster than most other types of landscape.

Wide open

Waves have the energy to change the coastline. Waves are caused by the wind. Their size depends on wind speed and how far they have travelled (Figure 1). This unbroken distance is called the **fetch**.

Waves and breakers

Water moves in a circle in a wave (Figure 2). In shallow water, friction from the sea bed slows down the bottom of the wave. The wave crest spills over as a **breaker**. Forward moving water from a breaker gives power to erode.

Tides

There is a **high** and a **low tide** twice every 12 hours 25 minutes. The difference between these heights is called the **tidal range** (Figure 3). The British Isles has a high tidal range compared to other parts of the world.

The highest range is during **spring** tides once every two weeks. **Neap** tides come between the spring tides. They have the lowest tidal range.

Ebb and flow

Fast local **currents** flow when the tide moves through a narrow stretch of water such as in estuaries and between islands. Currents give extra energy to erode and transport.

Figure 1 *The coast of Britain*

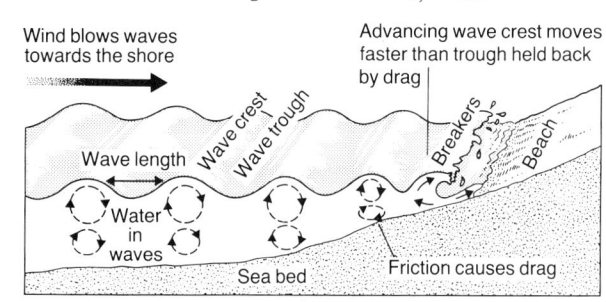

Figure 2 *Wave action*

	Tide heights for Dover UK on selected days		Tide heights for Sierra Leone on selected days	
	High water m	Low water m	High water m	Low water m
Day 1	5.2	0.4	2.4	1.1
	5.4	0.4	2.4	1.0
Day 2	5.4	0.2	3.3	0.2
	5.5	0.2	3.3	0.1
Day 3	5.6	0.1	3.4	0.1
	5.6	0	3.3	0.1
Day 4	5.7	0	3.4	0.1
	5.5	0.1	3.2	0.1

Figure 3 *Tide heights for Dover and Sierra Leone*

Exercises

1. Give two reasons why waves are likely to be more powerful along the south west peninsula of Britain than along the east coast.

2. Use Figure 2 to explain why breakers have power to cause erosion.

3. a Draw bar graphs of the tidal range for Dover and Sierra Leone.
   b Describe the differences you can see.
   c What is the difference between a spring and a neap tide.
   d Why does a high tidal range give more erosion along the coast?
   e Why do currents cause extra erosion?

Wave power

Waves erode by crashing tons of water onto a cliff (Figure 4). This is called **quarrying** or **hydraulic action**. The rock is weakened by shock waves as air is compressed in cracks. Pieces are broken off and washed away.

The broken pieces are thrown back against the cliff causing **abrasion**. The pieces themselves are broken down through **attrition** as they smash into each other. Rock is also eaten away by acids in the salt water.

Figure 4 *Cliff erosion*

Wearing back

Most erosion is at the cliff base. A notch or cave is cut out until the rock above collapses. In this way, the whole cliff face is worn back. The speed of erosion varies. It can be up to 6 m a year in clays, but is usually only a few cm in more resistant rocks.

As the cliff wears back, an area of flat rock is left at sea level. This is called a **wave cut platform**. The tides wash over it and plane it flat.

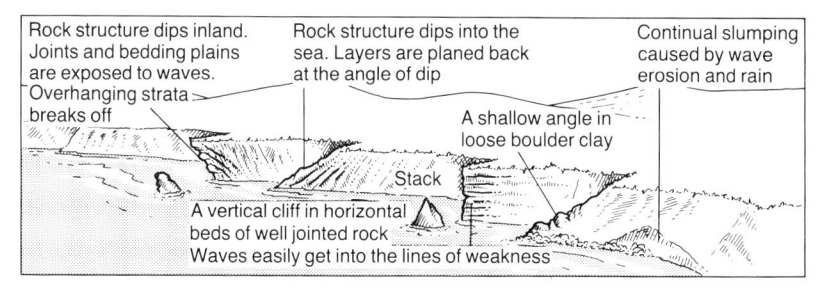

Figure 5 *Cliff profiles*

In profile

Soft rocks such as clays collapse at a shallow angle (Figure 5). Resistant rocks give more vertical cliffs. The rock structure also plays a part. Joints can be exposed or protected from wave attack depending on their angle.

Odd shapes

Arches are formed where waves break through joints in a headland (Figure 6). In time the arch collapses. The remaining piece is called a **stack**. These too are removed in time.

Figure 6 *An arch: the 'Green Bridge' in South Wales*

Exercises

4 Draw some sketches to illustrate the four ways that waves break up rock on a cliff. Add notes to explain what is happening, and how.

5 Use Figure 5 to draw cross-sections of different cliff profiles. Add labels and notes to explain the differences.

6 Explain how the feature in Figure 6 was formed, either with words or diagrams.

Beach billiards

Material eroded from the coast is taken away and **deposited** to form beaches. Waves break up a beach as the **swash**. Swash comes up the beach at an angle that depends on wind direction. Stones and sand are carried straight back down the beach in the **backwash**. This moves material in a zig-zag manner called **longshore drift** (Figure 7).

The swash Beach material washed up at an angle

The backwash Beach material is washed straight down the beach

Longshore drift Zig-zag movement of beach material along the shore

Waves approach at an angle

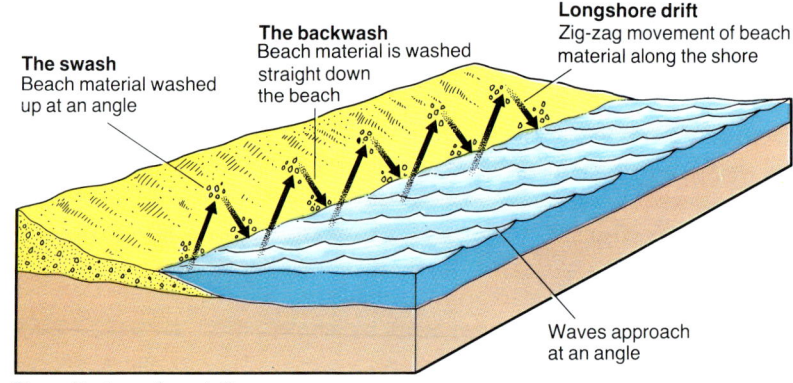

Figure 7 *Longshore drift*

Round the bend

As waves approach the shore, friction drags them round into a curve (Figure 8). This bending is called **wave refraction**.

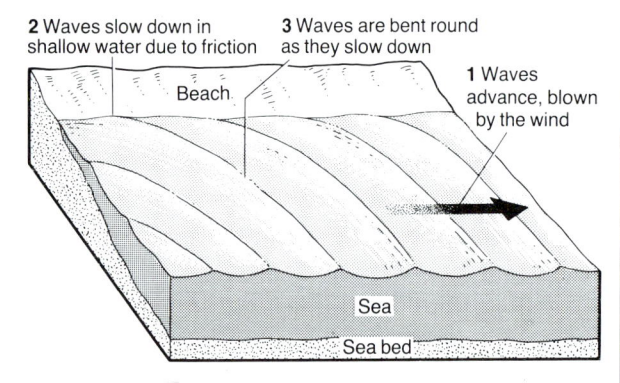

2 Waves slow down in shallow water due to friction
3 Waves are bent round as they slow down
1 Waves advance, blown by the wind
Beach
Sea
Sea bed

Figure 8 *Wave refraction*

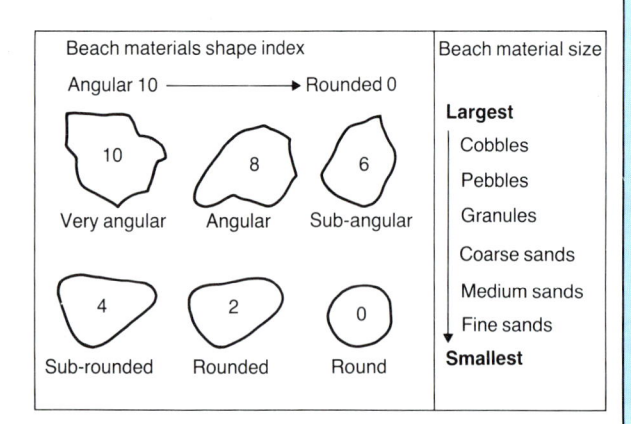

Beach materials shape index
Angular 10 → Rounded 0

10 Very angular
8 Angular
6 Sub-angular
4 Sub-rounded
2 Rounded
0 Round

Beach material size
Largest
Cobbles
Pebbles
Granules
Coarse sands
Medium sands
Fine sands
Smallest

Figure 9 *Pebble shapes*

On the beach

Beach material varies from fine muds and sands, to stones called **shingle**. There is fine sand where granite is nearby. In chalk areas, flint cobbles are more common. On most beaches, materials have come from many different places. These pieces soon become rounded by attrition, some more than others (Figure 9).

Exercises

7 a Make a copy of Figure 7.
   b Explain the title 'beach billiards'.
   c What could you do to find out how fast stones were moving along a beach?

8 a Why is there increased friction as a wave approaches the shore? (Hint: depth.)
   b How is the speed of longshore drift affected by wave refraction? (Hint: angle of swash.)

9 a What word is used to describe stones of different types and sizes on a beach?
   b Use Figure 9 to work out an index of roundness for these shapes:

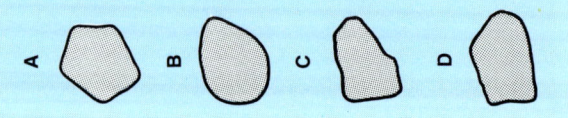

   A   B   C   D

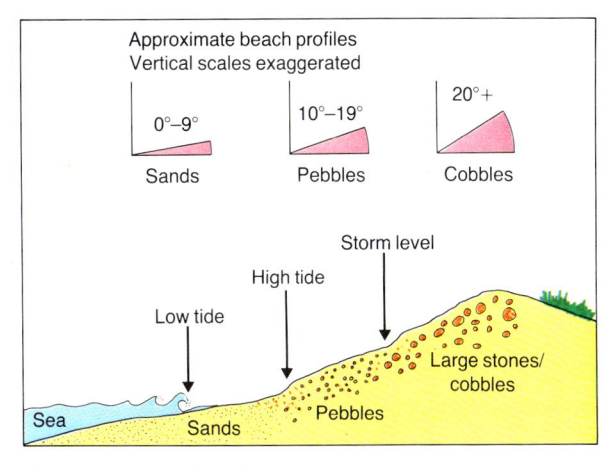

Figure 10 A beach profile

Figure 11 Sand dunes at Harlech

Beach profiles

The slope up a beach depends on the material it is made of (Figure 10). Large cobbles and pebbles give steep slopes while fine sand gives gentle slopes.

Some beaches rise in steps. The largest stones are washed to the top by the swash at high tide. A **storm ridge** shows where material was left after a storm. Finer material is washed back downslope by the less powerful backwash.

Dune building

Sand dunes sometimes form behind a wide sandy beach which dries out at low tide (Figure 11). Dry sand is blown back by onshore winds. More sand is trapped in marram grasses which can grow on the dunes. In time, the dune becomes **stabilized** as other vegetation takes root.

Muddy waters

There is also deposition in **estuaries** where rivers enter the sea (Figure 12). Much of the material is mud brought down in the rivers. Some is removed by **tidal scour**. The rest forms areas of **mud flats** which are covered over at high tide. Vegetation which can grow in salt water, such as eel grass and rice grass, helps trap more mud.

Figure 12 The Severn Estuary at low tide

New land

A **delta** may form where the river mud is not removed. The Mississippi Delta is one of the world's largest. About 135 million tonnes of mud is carried down the river each year. There is a low tidal range of 2 m in the Gulf of Mexico. This has allowed the delta to form.

Exercises

10 Describe how some beaches change from top to bottom. Mention:
   the materials they are made of
   the types of slope

11 Make a sketch of Figure 11. Add notes to explain how the sand dunes were formed.

12 a What are the signs in Figure 12 that deposition is taking place?
   b Why is there deposition in estuaries?
   c Why is there more deposition in some estuaries than in others?
   d Draw a map of the Mississippi or any one other major delta, such as the Nile or Ganges, from an atlas. Add notes to explain how it is formed.

Waves on the beach

Waves can either remove or build up a beach. Steep waves that break in quick succession have a weak swash (Figure 13). Backwash is stronger and drags material back down the beach. These are **destructive** waves that take material away.

Constructive waves are shallow with a strong swash (Figure 14). Backwash water has time to sink into the beach so is less powerful.

Shapes of deposition

Material is deposited in a variety of shapes. A **spit** is where sand or shingle builds up across an estuary or where the coast changes direction (Figure 15). A **bar** completely blocks the bay behind. A **tombola** is a beach which grows out to join an island. A shingle **foreland** forms where longshore drift from different directions brings material together to form a small headland.

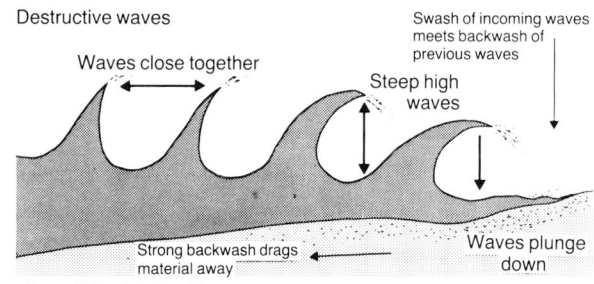

Figure 13 *Destructive waves*

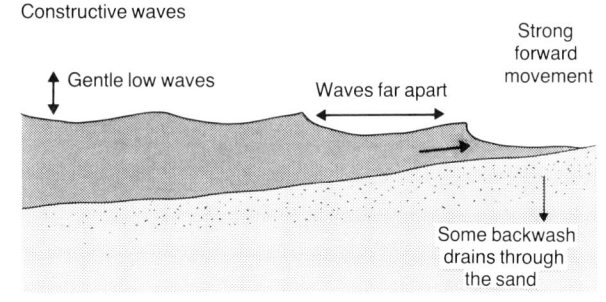

Figure 14 *Constructive waves*

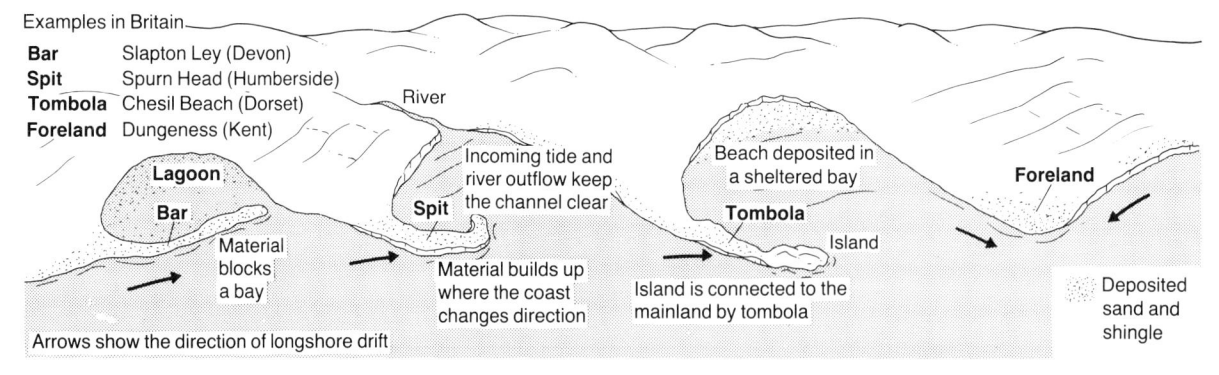

Examples in Britain
Bar Slapton Ley (Devon)
Spit Spurn Head (Humberside)
Tombola Chesil Beach (Dorset)
Foreland Dungeness (Kent)

Figure 15 *Features of deposition*

Exercises

13 Copy Figures 13 and 14 to show both destructive and constructive waves.

14 a What kind of weather would be most likely to give destructive waves?
   b Why are constructive waves more likely to be at the back of a shallow bay?

15 Draw three sets of sketches to show how:
   a a spit becomes a bar
   b a spit becomes a tombola
   c a shingle foreland is formed

16 Use an atlas to sketch and add notes about the coastal features at these places.
   a The Humber Estuary in Yorkshire UK.
   b The coast of Poland along the Baltic Sea.
   c The Texas coast in the Gulf of Mexico.

Figure 16 *The Sandy Hook spit near New York*

Rapid change

The coastline can change very quickly. Storms can break up a beach within a few hours. Coastlines have been worn back by several kilometres within only a few hundred years.

Deposition features, such as spits, continually change shape as loose sand and shingle is moved on (Figure 16).

Links

Change in one place affects other parts of the coast (Figure 17). Deposition stops when the supply of eroded material stops. A new feature, such as a spit, causes changes in local currents. Areas of slack water become **lagoons** where mud and vegetation collects.

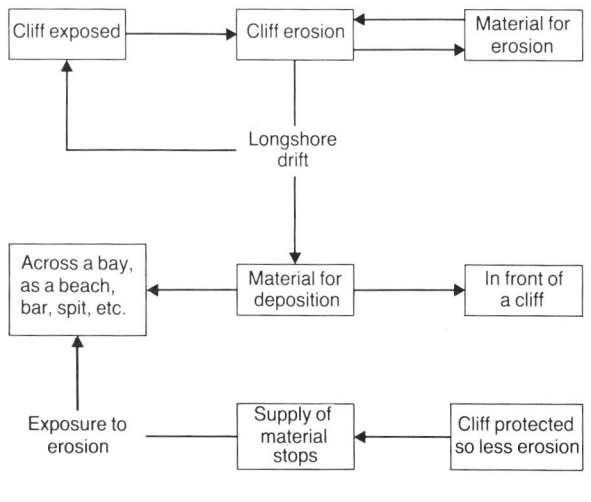

Figure 17 *Links between processes*

Exercises

17 Study Figure 16.
  a How can you tell that the main wind direction is from the right of the photo?
  b About how wide is the spit at both its widest and narrowest points? Use at the road as a guide to scale.
  c How can you tell where the ends of the spit used to be?

18 Study Figure 17.
  a Explain how erosion in one place is linked to deposition somewhere else.
  b How can deposition slow down erosion?

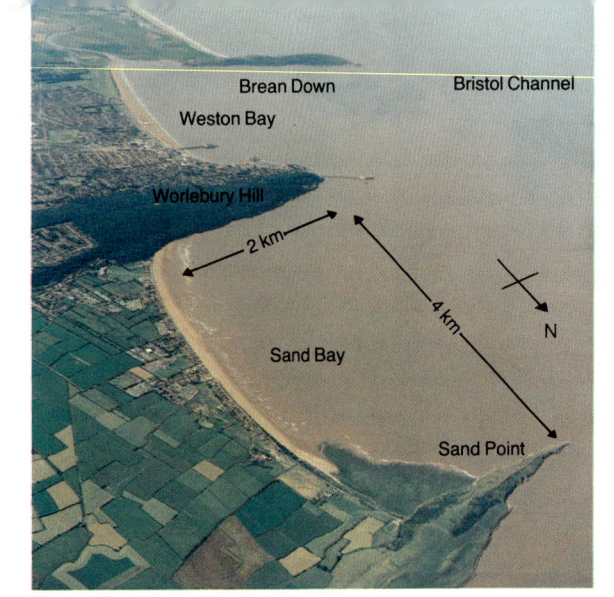

Figure 18 *Weston Bay in Avon*

Erosion by steps

Headlands are always exposed to wave attack. A bay is only eroded while waves with enough energy can reach the back (Figure 20). As a bay is eroded back, the waves must travel further over shallow sheltered water. Energy is lost and erosion stops.

There can be no more erosion until the headlands have worn back further. This allows more powerful waves to reach the back again.

Attacking the weak

Bays and **headlands** form where different rocks are being eroded by the sea (Figure 18). Some rocks are **resistant** to erosion. They may be hard, have few joints, or lines of weakness are not exposed to the waves. Softer and more exposed rocks are more easily eroded. The less resistant rocks are worn back to form bays. More resistant rocks form headlands (Figure 19).

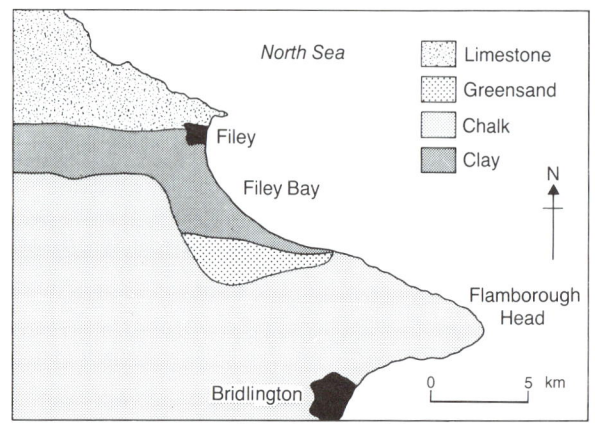

Figure 19 *The geology of Filey Bay in Yorkshire*

Exercises

19 a Describe the coastline shown in Figure 18.
    b Suggest reasons for the shape of the coastline. Use ideas from Figure 19 to help.

20 a Use Figure 20 to describe clearly how a bay wears backwards. Divide your answer into these separate stages:
        strong headland and bay erosion
        strong headland erosion, weak bay erosion
        strong headland erosion, increasing bay erosion
    b Draw a map to show how you think Filey Bay might change as the bay is eroded back.

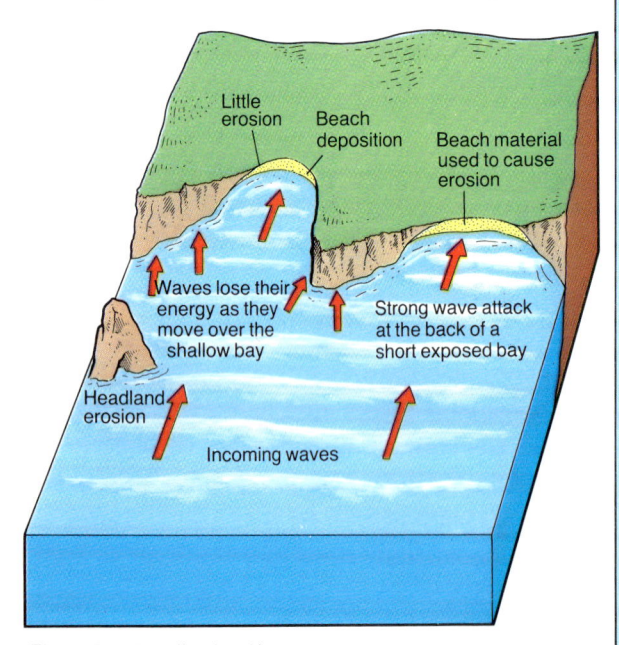

Figure 20 *Headland and bay erosion*

A lot to learn

There is still a lot to learn about how coastal features are formed. An idea called a **hypothesis** is needed first (Figure 21). Then facts are collected to describe the feature. Next, the hypothesis can be tested to see if it fits the facts.

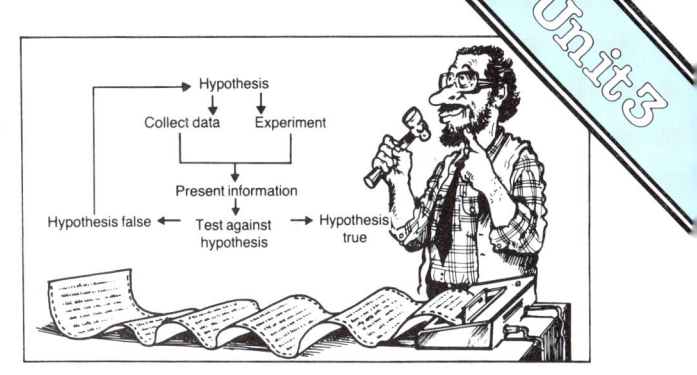

Figure 21 *Testing a hypothesis*

The Chesil puzzle

Chesil Beach is a puzzle (Figure 22). The beach material is mostly shingle with pebbles of limestone, flint, sandstone, granite and many others (Figure 23). One hypothesis is that longshore drift brought them along the coast from the west where these rocks are found. If this is true, the larger pebbles should be on the western end.

In fact, pebbles at the eastern end are larger (Figure 24)! Perhaps this means the beach has been built up from material driven onshore from the sea bed. The water is deeper at this end so the waves are more powerful.

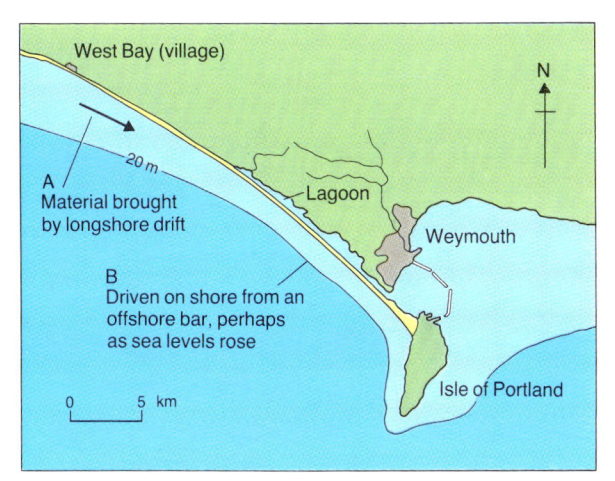

Figure 22 *Chesil Beach*

Figure 23 *Stones on Chesil Beach*

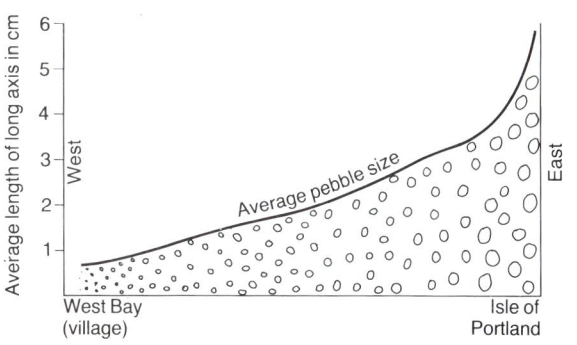

Figure 24 *Stone size on Chesil Beach*

Exercises

21 a What is a hypothesis?
    b Why is fieldwork needed to see if a hypothesis is true?

22 Use Figures 22, 23 and 24, with an atlas geology map, to answer these questions.
    a Explain why the beach material has probably come from the west.
    b Why would the larger pebbles be at the western end if longshore drift was from the west?
    c What does Figure 24 show about the size of beach materials?
    d How might the depth of offshore water affect the size of pebbles that are thrown up on Chesil Beach? Think about how powerful the waves might be.
    e Give reasons why any hypothesis about the origin of the beach is hard to prove.

3.5 Planning the coast

Surfers use waves from Cornwall to California. Breakers spill over and rush forward as waves reach shallow water. Waves can be fun! (Figure 1).

Watts new

Waves may also be an answer to future **energy** supplies. The motion up and down can be linked to an electric generator (Figure 2). Up to 20 per cent of the UK's energy needs could come from the large waves west of the Hebrides (Figure 3). The fetch and wind speed here makes this possible.

Figure 1 *Surfing*

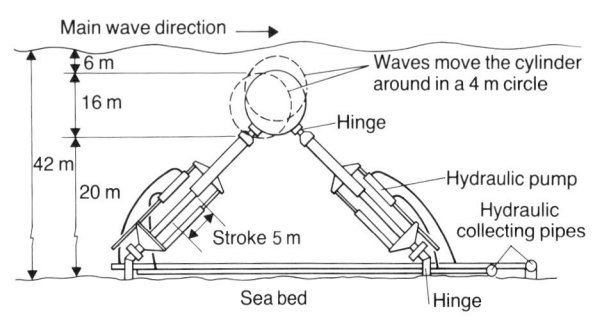

Figure 2 *The Bristol Cylinder*

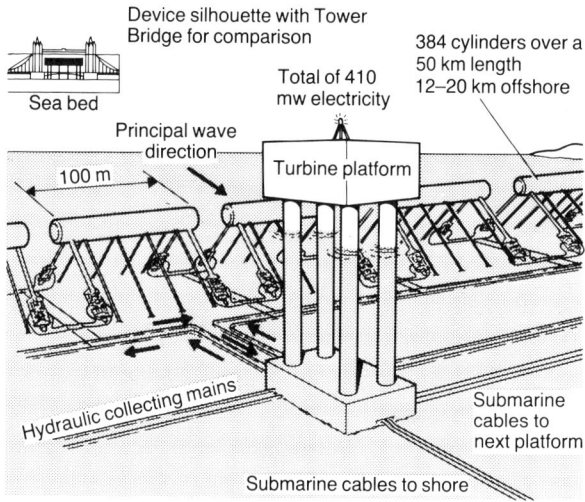

Figure 3 *Energy from the waves*

Turning the tides

In the Rance Estuary in Brittany, the tide turns turbines built into a barrage. This gives electricity without using up resources.

A similar scheme is planned in the Severn Estuary (Figure 4). If built, the scheme could give 10 per cent of total UK energy needs.

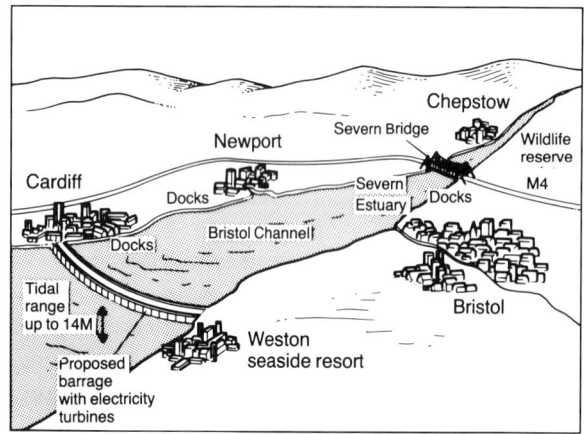

Figure 4 *A Severn Barrage Scheme*

Exercises

1. Make a list of occupations and activities where information about waves is needed.

2. What do you think about the idea shown in Figures 2 and 3? Mention these things:
   - the design of the scheme
   - problems it might cause
   - waves as a source of energy

3. Study Figure 4. Find another large estuary in the British Isles. Design a tidal barrage scheme. Write a report to describe the advantages and problems of the scheme. Think about these things:
   - new energy supplies
   - new roads
   - changes to shipping
   - effects on estuary wildlife

Save our beach

A good beach is the main attraction at **seaside resorts**. A sandy beach is best, but even shingle will do. Keeping the beach is often a problem. Longshore drift moves it from place to place.

Wood or concrete walls called **groynes** are one solution (Figure 5). They trap the material at least for a few more years.

The Dutch coast

About 10 per cent of the Netherlands is below sea level. Sand dunes form a natural defence against the sea along much of the coast (Figure 6). However, they must be protected against erosion both by the sea, and by people.

Figure 5 *A beach groyne*

Dune defence

Planting trees and grasses is one way to do this. The roots bind the sand and trap new sand. Groynes keep beaches in place. This gives the dunes a constant supply of sand and also protects them from wave erosion. Using nature in this way is often the best solution.

Sea walls called **dykes** have been built where the dunes are too low. Care must also be taken not to let the water table sink too low. This would let the dunes dry out and be blown away.

Figure 6 *The Dutch dune coast*

Exercises

4 Use Figure 5 to explain how a groyne helps stop longshore drift.

5 a Why is the Dutch coast so open to wind and waves? Measure the fetch across the North Sea. Say where the main wind comes from.
   b Why is protecting the dunes so important?
   c Explain how people cause erosion to the sand dunes.
   d Draw a cross-section from the sea to the inland flat land to illustrate the different ways the dunes are being protected.

Barton's sea view

The 'sea view' is getting too close for comfort at Barton on Sea (Figure 7). Houses have already been demolished as the cliff is worn back (Figure 8). Stopping the erosion is a problem that engineers have often tried to solve.

Figure 7 *The bay at Barton on Sea*

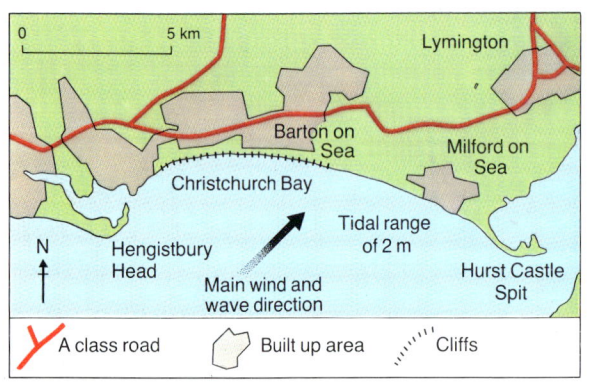

Figure 8 *Christchurch Bay*

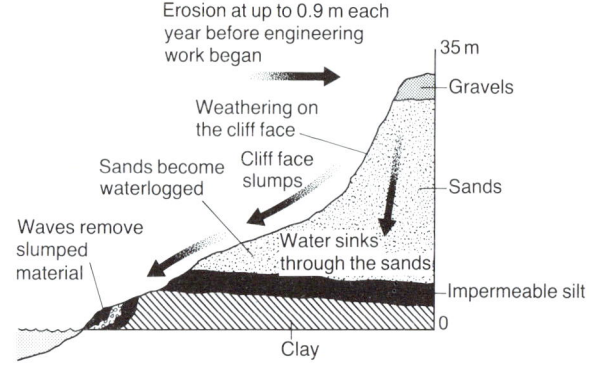

Figure 9 *Geology of the cliff*

Cliff collapse

The problem is caused by the rocks that make up the cliff (Figure 9). Soft sands and gravels lie above a layer of fine clay called silt. The silt is impermeable so water cannot sink through the cliff. Instead, the sands and gravels above become lubricated with rainwater. Eventually the cliff face collapses in a **slump** (Figure 10).

Waves which reach the back of Christchurch Bay still have most of their energy. They remove the slumped material and expose the cliff to even more erosion.

Figure 10 *Cliff erosion*

Exercises

6 a How high is the cliff at Barton on Sea?
   b About how close are the nearest buildings to the cliff edge?
   c What was the rate of cliff erosion before the defence work?

7 Write a geological report on the causes of cliff erosion at Barton on Sea. Include some diagrams. Use these headings.
   The geology of the cliff
   Causes of slumping
   Wave erosion

Unit 3

Figure 11 labels:
- Stone groyne to break up incoming waves
- Slope made more shallow to keep stable
- Stone blocks to stop wave attack reaching sands and gravels
- Wall of interlocking steel sheets to stop slumping

Figure 11 *Coastal defences*

Figure 12 *Danger spots*

Figure 13 *Buildings at risk*

Steel and rock walls

Hard limestone blocks have been piled up to stop wave attack on the soft sands and gravels (Figure 11). Groynes have been built to break up the waves as they come onshore.

Steel walls sunk vertically into the ground to stop slumping are soon pushed over and bent out of shape. Drains have been laid to take water out of the cliff before it becomes waterlogged. Some sections of beach have been flattened and the slope made more stable.

Buying time

Homes and businesses along the cliff top are under threat (Figures 12, 13). Already, over £1 million has been spent protecting the cliff at Barton. About £70 000 is spent every year maintaining the defences. This must be paid for out of local council and water rates.

Nothing seems to work for long. Steel and stones are no match for wind, water and waves.

Exercises

8   Draw a large sketch of Figure 11. Label in the different ways engineers have tried to stop cliff erosion.

9   a How might the groynes help stop cliff erosion? Mention:
       the direction of wind and waves
       trapping beach material
    b What signs are there that the steel walls do not stop slumping?
    c How can stone blocks stop erosion?
    d Explain how changing the angle of cliff slope can reduce erosion.
    e Why might better drainage reduce erosion?

10 What do you think each of the following people might want to say about sea defences at Barton?
       The owner of the building in Figure 13
       Ratepayers in other parts of Hampshire
       A professional civil engineer
       A local government councillor

London's sinking feeling

Before 1985, central London was under an increasing risk of being flooded. The weight of buildings on soft rocks beneath is causing the city to sink (Figure 14). New wharves and marsh reclamation along the Thames Estuary now stop natural flooding near the sea. This means that high water levels are funnelled upstream to London itself.

North Sea low

The greatest danger has been when an area of low pressure passes over the North Sea (Figure 15). Strong northerly winds cause the sea to **surge** towards the south and up the river estuaries.

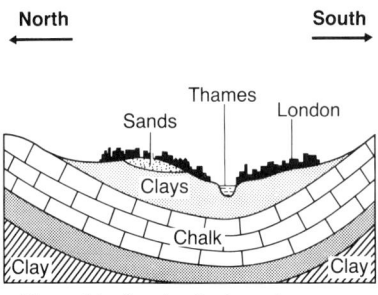

Figure 14 *London Basin geology*

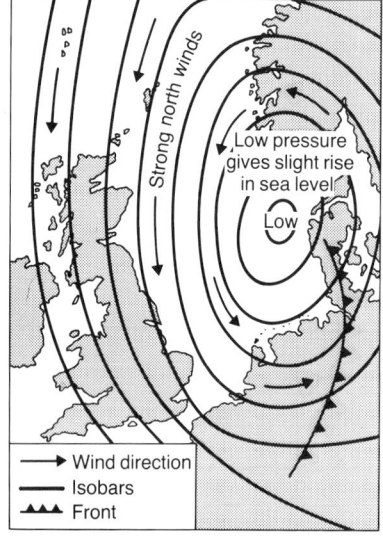

Figure 15 *Depression over the North Sea*

Thames gates

The solution has been to build the Thames Barrier (Figures 16, 17). A smaller barrier at Barking Creek has also been needed. These will not stop the city sinking or the North Sea rising. However, they will hold back flooding for a while at least.

Figure 16 *The Thames Barrier*

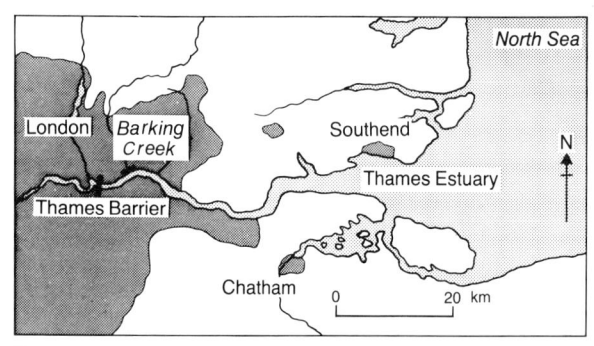

Figure 17 *The Thames Estuary*

Vanishing marshlands

As well as their use to prevent flooding, coastal marshlands have rare vegetation and wildlife. These **habitats** are under threat as more land is being **reclaimed** for other uses. Conservation is needed or this unique ecosystem will be lost forever.

Exercises

12 Explain how both of these things meant that flooding in central London had become more likely:
    geology
    building docks downstream

13 Write a short weather report to describe why there might be an especially high tide in the Thames Estuary and on the Essex coast.

14 Sketch Figure 16. Add notes to describe what it is and how it works.

UNIT 4 The big freeze

4.1 Introduction

It is hard to picture Britain under ice, sand, or even under water. Yet Britain has been affected by all these things at times when the climate was different from today.

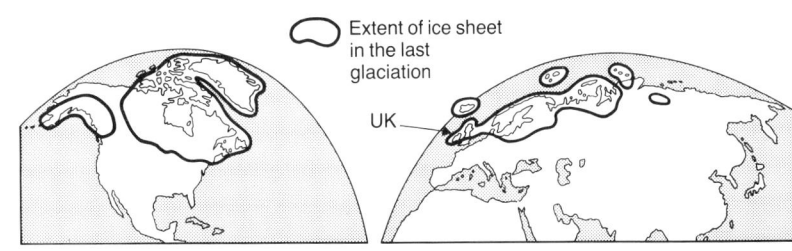

Figure 1   *The Ice Age in the Northern Hemisphere*

Ice age Earth

About 400 000 years ago, the climate in many parts of the world became very cold and ice began to spread (Figure 1). An ice sheet 800 m thick covered central Wales while the Isle of Man was buried under 1600 m. The period known as the **Ice Age** had begun.

Warm and cold periods

The climate in the Ice Age was not always cold. In Britain there were three very cold periods called **glacials** (Figure 2). Each lasted about 100 000 years. They were separated by warmer times

Figure 2   *Glacial conditions*

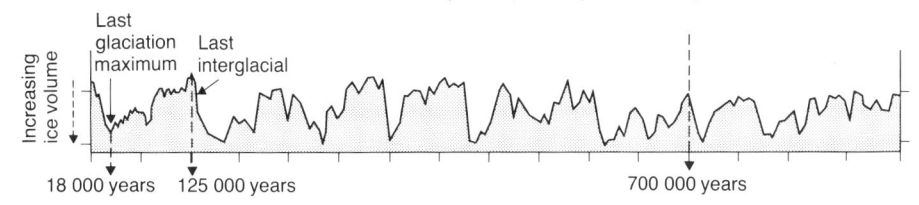

Figure 3   *Inter-glacials of the Ice Age*

called **inter-glacials** when the ice melted (Figure 3). Each inter-glacial lasted about 10 000 years.

The last glacial period ended 10 000 years ago. Some scientists think that we are still in an inter-glacial period. The next Ice Age is coming!

A cold planet

Ice Ages are quite common. There have been 21 in the past two million years. In some ways Earth is still a 'cold' planet. In the northern hemisphere winter, half of the land and a third of the oceans are covered with snow and ice.

Exercises

1. a When did the last Ice Age begin?
    b How many cold periods were there in Britain?
    c State two differences between a glacial and an inter-glacial period.

2. Use Figure 1 and an atlas to name five countries which were covered by an ice sheet.

3. State one fact to show the ice was very thick.

4.2 Ice on the move

Many landscapes were shaped during the Ice Age. When the ice moved it eroded powerfully. New landforms were created.

From snow to ice

Snow rather than rain fell during the glacial periods. Great thicknesses built up in **snowfields** in the mountains. The bottom layers were compressed, the air squeezed out and **glacial ice** formed. In Western Europe the change from snow to ice took beween 25 and 100 years.

The ice spreads

In some places the ice buried high land completely in a thick sheet called an **ice cap**. Only the highest peaks stuck through the ice as **nunataks**. Some ice accumulated in large mountain hollows called **corries**. Eventually the ice overflowed and moved down valleys as **valley glaciers** (Figure 1).

Figure 1 *Muldrow Glacier*

Figure 2 *Origins of moraines*

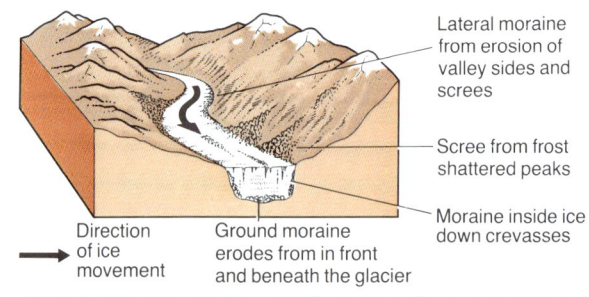

The Muldrow Glacier

The Muldrow Glacier begins at a height of 5500 m in the Alaska Range. It is 66 km long and up to 475 m thick. Like most glaciers in the world the Muldrow is usually stagnant and was much larger during the Ice Age.

When the glacier moved it collected vast quantities of boulders, stones, sand and soil called **moraine** (Figure 2 and 3). The moraine was eroded from the sides and floor of the valley. The screes lining the valley in Figure 1 show that today most moraine falls onto the ice from the surrounding frost-shattered peaks.

Figure 3 *Moraine at the base of a glacier*

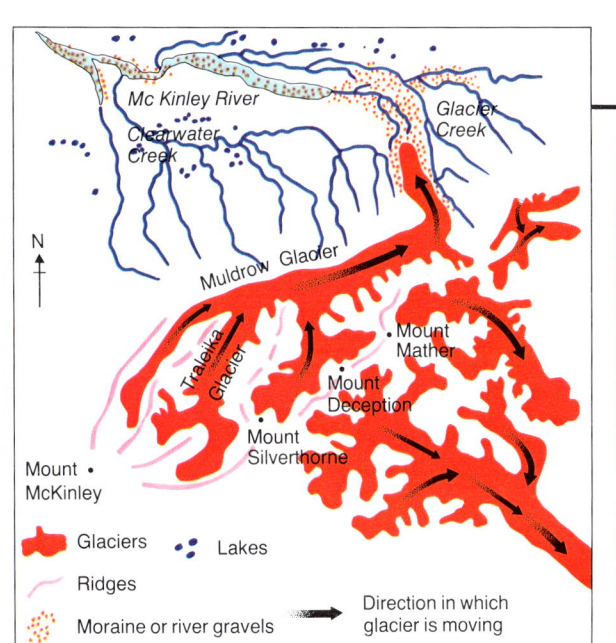

Figure 4 *Muldrow Glacier and its tributaries*

Figure 5 *Mer de Glace, glacier in France*

Plastic ice

Muldrow is fed by several tributary glaciers (Figure 4). If more ice is fed in than is melting, the glacier moves forward. In a glacial period, the Muldrow would probably have moved at a speed of a metre each day.

The ice behaved like plastic and oozed forward. The ice crystals were deformed by the great weight of ice pressing on top and from behind. The glacier would also have moved as a result of slipping and sliding.

The surface of the glacier is split by cracks called **crevasses** (Figure 5). These have been caused by the pressure of the ice, uneven valley floor and friction against rock.

Melting away

Most glaciers in the world begin melting in summer. **Meltwater streams** flow from beneath the ice. Glacier Creek and the McKinley River flow from the Muldrow Glacier. The glacier here is a mass of melting ice and heaps of moraine (Figure 4).

Exercises

1. a Make a copy of Figure 6.
   Match up these features with their correct letter.
   Use Figure 1 to help you.
   corrie ... valley glacier ... moraine ... ridge ... snowfield ... screes ... nunatak
   b Explain what each feature is.

2. Write a description of the Muldrow Glacier. Mention: how the ice forms ... how it moves ... tributary glaciers ... its size ... melting.

3. Make your own sketch of Figure 5. Label on it as many glacial features as you can.

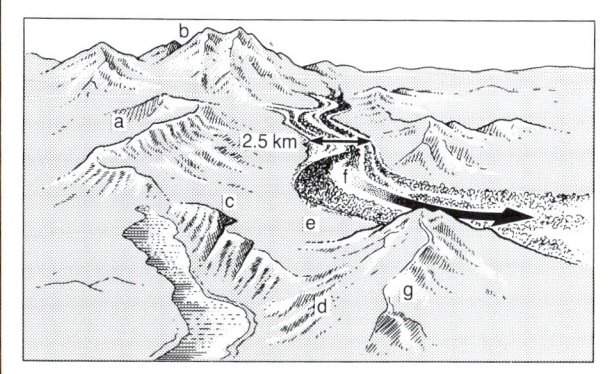

Figure 6 *A sketch of the Muldrow Glacier*

Figure 7 *The Canadian Shield landscape, studded with lakes*

The landscape carve-up

Today, vast areas of Canada and Scandinavia are dotted with lakes, bare rock and small rocky hills (Figure 7). These lowlands were shaped by ice sheets. In the Canadian shield, the weathered rock on the surface was about 10 m thick. The ice has stripped this off.

Erosion by ice

Ice erodes the land by **quarrying** (**plucking**) (Figure 8). This is done in two ways.

Ice at the base of the glacier melts in the summer thaw or because of the tremendous pressure of ice. The water then freezes in joints and breaks off blocks by frost shattering. Moving ice removes the pieces. Quarrying also takes place when a glacier freezes on solid rock. Rock is plucked out as it moves along.

Glaciers also erode by **abrasion** (Figure 8). Rocks in the base and sides of the ice scrape against the land surface and erode it.

Scratching and smoothing

Grooves in the rock called **striations** are scratched by boulders in the base of the ice (Figure 9). Finer material rubs on rock surfaces and makes them smooth.

Roches moutonnées owe their shape to the plucking and smoothing effects of ice (Figure 10). They are hillocks of more resistant rock. The ice smooths the upflow side but plucks out a jagged face on the downflow side by quarrying and abrasion (Figure 10).

Figure 8 *Quarrying and abrasion*

Figure 9 *Striations on solid rock*

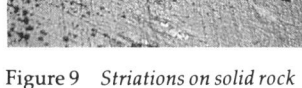

Figure 10 *Roche moutonnée in North Wales*

Lakes carved in rock

The ice gouged out hollows where there were weaknesses in the rock (Figure 11). Some weaknesses resulted from pressure release joints formed when the ice stripped off the surface rock layers. Some rocks in front of the ice were shattered by frost action. When the glaciers melted **rock basin lakes** filled the hollows (Figure 12).

Ice thickens in hollows, speeds up, erosion more powerful

Pressure release joints on steps where ice is thinner
Made jagged by **quarrying**

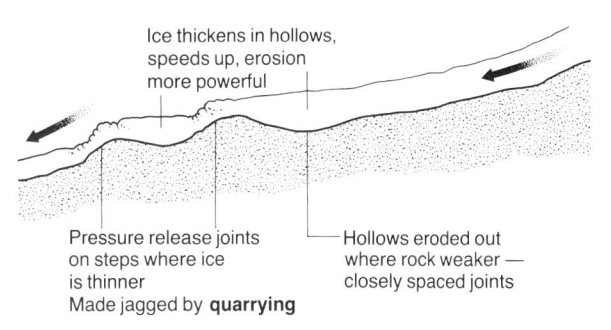

Hollows eroded out where rock weaker — closely spaced joints

Figure 11 *Formation of rock steps and lakes*

Exercises

4 a Describe the scenery in Figure 12 and explain how it was formed. Use these words:
      ice-scoured lowland ... quarrying ... abrasion ... rock basin lakes ... the number of lakes ... hills
   b Why do you think the hills in the distance remain?

5 Make a labelled sketch of Figure 10. Mark where striations might be found.

Figure 12 *Glaciated lowland in North West Scotland*

Figure 13 *U-shaped valley*

Deep valleys in high lands

Some ice flowed along existing valleys. These valley glaciers widened and deepened the valleys into **U-shaped troughs** up to a kilometre wide and several hundred metres deep (Figure 13).

Tributary valleys were left high up on the valley sides as **hanging valleys**. The great size of the valley glaciers gave them the power to carve a straighter route through the land (Figure 14). Ridges of land were cut back to form **truncated spurs**.

Fed by tributaries

Many glaciers were fed by smaller glaciers flowing out of tributary valleys (Figure 14). These tributary glaciers increased the erosive power of the main glacier. They helped carve very deep U-shaped valleys.

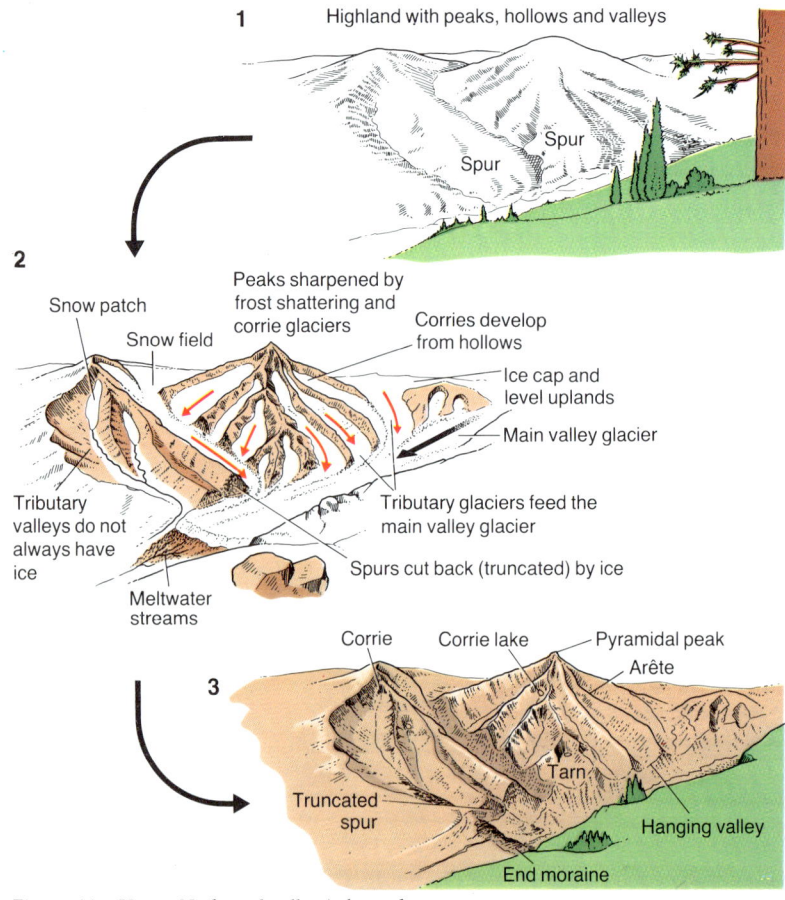

Figure 14 *How a U-shaped valley is formed*

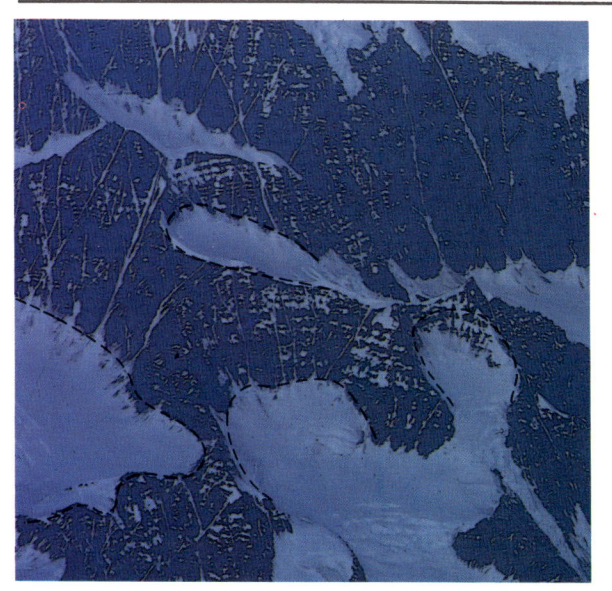

Figure 15 *A corrie*

Figure 16 *A pyramidal peak in Norway*

Hollows in the hills

The hollows called corries were carved by **corrie glaciers** (Figure 15). Snow which later became ice built up in hollows on the sides of mountains. These hollows were deepened and widened as the ice spilled out of them. It moved out as a corrie glacier.

Where a mountain had several corries, it became sharpened into a **pyramidal peak** (Figure 16). Narrow ridges called **arêtes** were formed as two corries eroded towards each other (Figure 17).

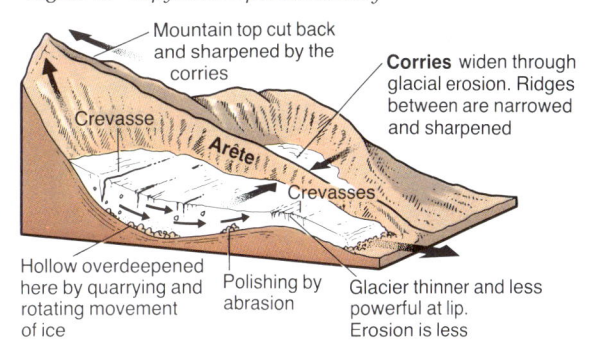

Figure 17 *How a corrie and pyramidal peak are formed*

Exercises

6 a Make a sketch of Figure 13. Label on these glacial features:
   U-shape ... flat valley floor ... hanging valley ... truncated spurs
   b Describe how the ice made such a deep valley. Mention how tributary glaciers would help.

7 Put the following into the correct order of events. Use Figures 14 and 17 to help you.

the land between corries is sharpened into an arête and pyramidal peak
the back wall is steepened
corries on the same mountain will wear backwards towards each other
the ice erodes by quarrying and abrasion
snow in the hollows is compressed into ice
the ice thickens and spills out of the hollow
the enlarged hollow is called a corrie
snow builds up in a hollow on a mountain
as the ice moves out it erodes
the erosion deepens and widens the hollow

8 Make labelled sketches of Figures 15 and 16.

4.3 Danger from ice

Glaciers and ice sheets lock up a vast amount of energy. Once released, the energy can cause widespread damage to people and property.

Glacial hazards

People living in the Chamonix Valley in France have a long history of danger from the Mer de Glace glacier (Figure 1). Lives have been at risk from the moving glacier and the melting ice which floods along the **meltwater streams**.

Most glaciers are in remote mountain areas so when they move or melt few people are affected.

Ice dangers

There are several types of **glacial hazard**. The main danger today is from **ice avalanches**. Glaciers have melted back so much that some hang on the top of the steep valley sides. They seem ready to fall at any time (Figure 2).

Surging ice

Sometimes glaciers move forward rapidly without warning as an **ice surge**. This can be caused by earthquakes or extra heavy snowfall.

A more usual reason is when snowfall thickens ice in the upper part of a glacier. This puts pressure on the lower part until the whole glacier becomes unstable. The pressure is released by the glacier surging forward and loose ice piles up near the snout (Figure 3).

Dates	Events
1600	Advancing glaciers destroy 7 houses in the Argentière-La Rosière area.
1610	Torrents from the Bossons glacier severely damage Le Fouilly.
1613 or 1614	Glacial meltwater completes the destruction of La Bonneville.
1616	About 6 houses remaining at Le Châtelard. Between 1642–1700 the village was abandoned.
1628–30	Flooding of the Arve due to glacial meltwater.
1640s	Glaciers came close to Le Tour, Argentière, La Rosière, Les Tines, Les Bois, Les Praz and Les Boissons. 1641: avalanche of snow and ice destroyed 2 homes at Le Tour and killed 4 cows and 8 sheep. 1641–43: property flooded and ruined by torrents from the Bossons glacier.
1730	Mer de Glace less than 400 m from the nearest houses at Les Bois.
1818–1820	Glaciers again almost at Le Tour, Montquart and Les Bois.
1826	Mer de Glace showering debris onto the chalets below.
1835	Ice blocks from the Mer de Glace threaten to fall on Les Bois.
1852	Several glacier avalanches in the Chamonix valley due to warm winds and heavy rains.
1878	Sudden torrents of water from the Mer de Glace.
1949	Ice avalanche kills 6 people.
1977	Village threatened by ice avalanche.

Figure 1 *Glacial hazards at Chamonix*

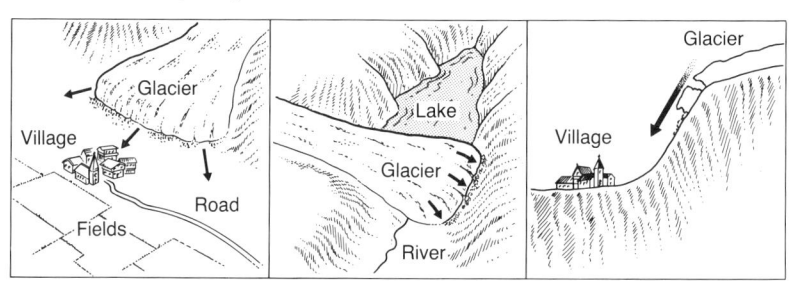

Figure 2 *Glacial hazards*

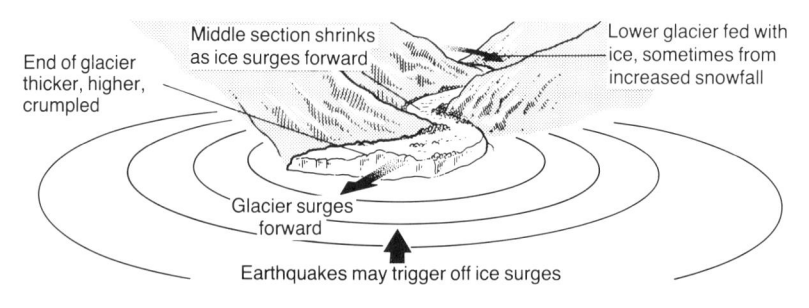

Figure 3 *Ice surge*

Exercises

1. Study Figure 1.
   List three dangers each from ice and meltwater in the Arve Valley.

2. a Sketch three types of glacial hazard.
   b Why is the damage they cause limited?

3. What may happen if the upper part of a glacier thickens? Why?

Himalayan highway

The Karakoram Highway winds through the Himalayas linking Kashmir with China (Figure 4). As it snakes its way around 7000 m high peaks, the highway is in danger from avalanches, ice surges and floods.

The Ghulkin menace

The Ghulkin Glacier is 450 m thick and has a steep gradient of 1 in 3.7. It has huge tension crevasses which are 30 m wide and 100 m deep (Figure 5).

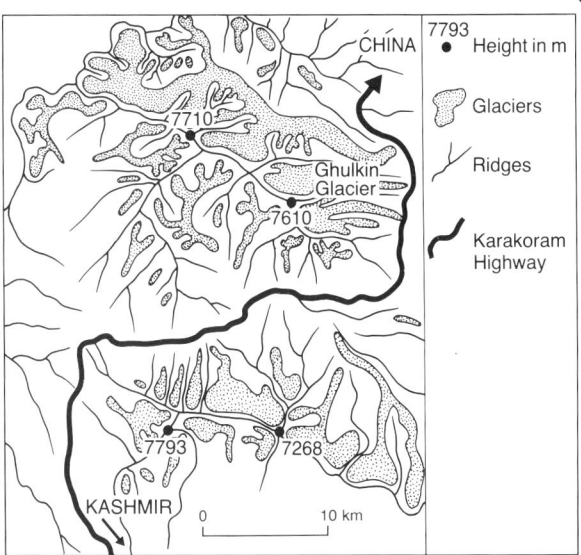

Figure 4 *The Karakoram Highway*

Figure 5 *Ghulkin Glacier*

Figure 6 *The Karakoram Highway flooded by meltwater from the Ghulkin Glacier*

Meltwater damage

It was the meltwater river of the Ghulkin Glacier which was the danger in 1980. It changed course, flooded the Karakoram Highway and buried it in a large fan of boulders (Figure 6).

The river started to change course while under the Ghulkin Glacier. The melting of the ice and the dumping of its moraine made a new route.

Exercise

4 Write a civil engineer's report about the blocking of the Karakoram Highway. Think of a suitable headline.
Mention: the type of landscape the road goes through ... the danger from the Ghulkin Glacier ... the meltwater river changes course. Illustrate your report.

4.4 Frozen hard

Today, one-fifth of the world's land surface has frozen ground. These areas are some of the most barren and inhospitable places on earth.

Land near the ice

During the Ice Age, land near the glaciers and ice sheets was frozen hard. Southern Britain was like this during the cold periods. These kinds of places are called **periglacial** areas. The landscape is known as **tundra**.

Today they are mainly on land around the Arctic Ocean (Figure 1). Ground may be frozen to depths of hundreds of metres. This frozen ground is called **permafrost**.

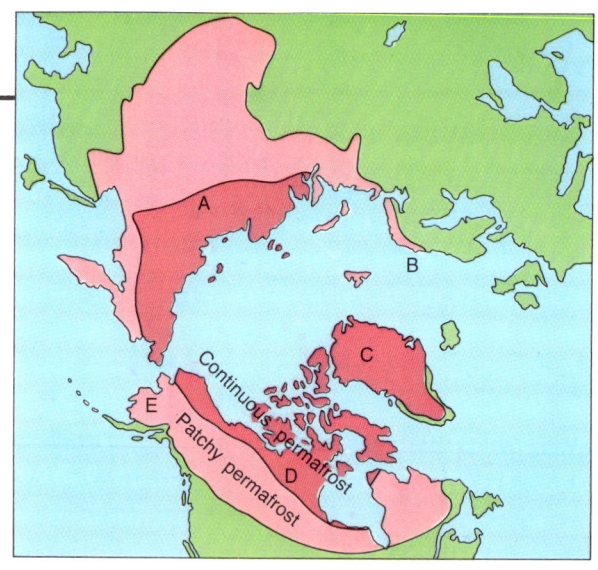

Figure 1 *Permafrost in the Northern Hemisphere*

Thawing out

The top three to six metres of the permafrost thaws out in summer. This is the **active layer**. It is a mixture of stones, rocks, sands and clayey material formed by frost breaking up the surface.

Patterns on the ground

Aerial views of the tundra often show a pattern of hundreds of lakes (Figure 2). The lakes form where the ground thaws and subsides in summer. Some lakes fill hollows made by **ice wedges** (Figure 3). These wedges fill the polygonal cracks made when the active layer freezes and contracts in winter. They push up the ground to form the rim of the lakes.

Figure 2 *Polygonal patterned lakes*

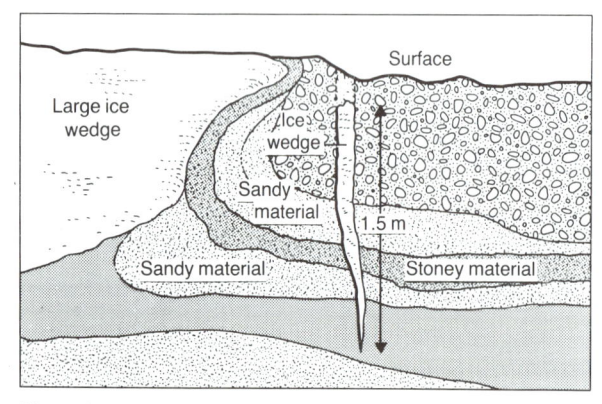

Figure 3 *Ice wedges*

Exercises

1. a Make a trace of Figure 1.
   b Use an atlas to label on the names of countries A to E with permafrost.

2. Sort out these pairs.
   cracks in active layer / lakes filled with ice
   the top of permafrost / permafrost which thaws
   covering much of the / tundra
   land after the
   summer thaw
   ground often frozen / active layer
   to great depths
   land near glaciers / ice wedges
   and ice sheets

Heaving and pushing

When the water in the active layer freezes it pushes the ground up into hummocks. This is called **frost heaving**. Stones and rocks cool down more rapidly than other parts of the active layer. As a result lenses of ice form under them.

Frost heaving by the lenses pushes the stones to the surface. They may become sorted into shapes such as circles (Figure 4). These areas of sorted stones are called **patterned ground**.

Eskimo hills

Hills over 60 m high rise above the flat tundra in Canada (Figure 5). They are called **pingoes** after the Eskimo name for a hill. It is not certain why they form. They develop in areas where the active layer has plenty of water. The beds of former lakes are an example. The water freezes into a huge lens of ice which pushes up the ground into a hill. The pingo has a core of ice even in summer.

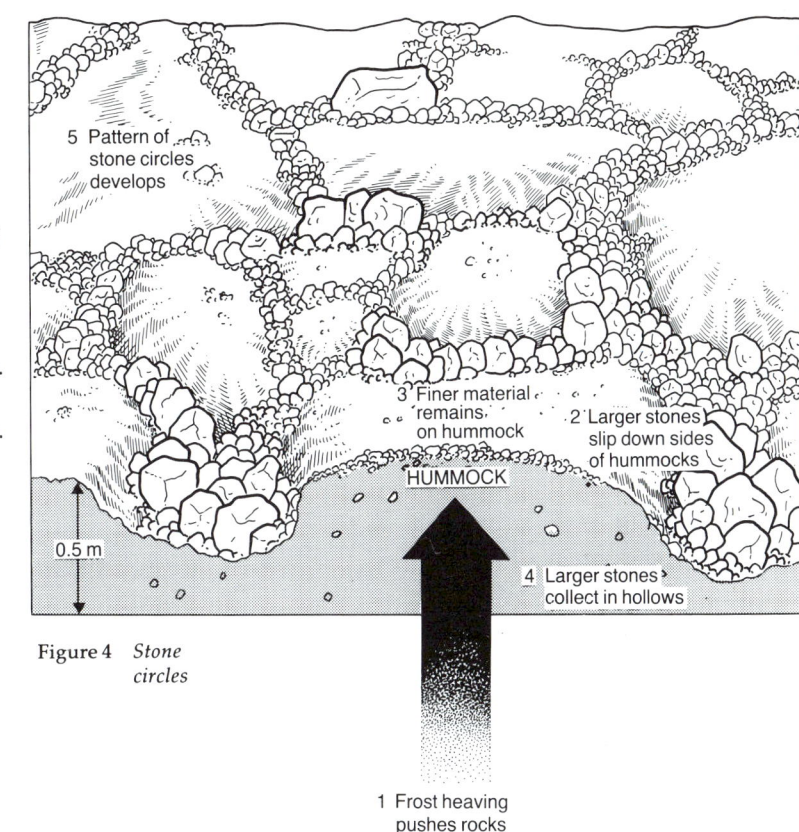

Figure 4 *Stone circles*

5 Pattern of stone circles develops
3 Finer material remains on hummock
2 Larger stones slip down sides of hummocks
HUMMOCK
0.5 m
4 Larger stones collect in hollows
1 Frost heaving pushes rocks to surface

Figure 5 *A pingo*

Exercises

3 Study Figure 4.
   a Why is the ground hummocky?
   b In what way are the stones sorted?
   c Describe how this happens.

4 a Make a labelled sketch of Figure 5.
   b Why are pingoes only found in certain places?

Living with permafrost

Rock-hard permafrost and the thawing of its surface in summer create many problems. Few people live in the Canadian North but large sums of money have to be spent on the construction of homes and services. Engineers have to build the foundations of pipes, roads and buildings carefully.

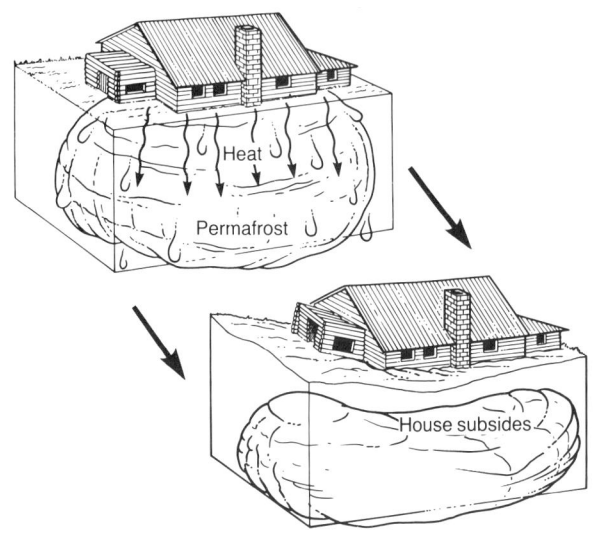

Figure 6 *Heat from a house causes thawing and subsidence*

Moving ground

In Figure 6 heat from the house thawed the permafrost. The house subsided and collapsed.

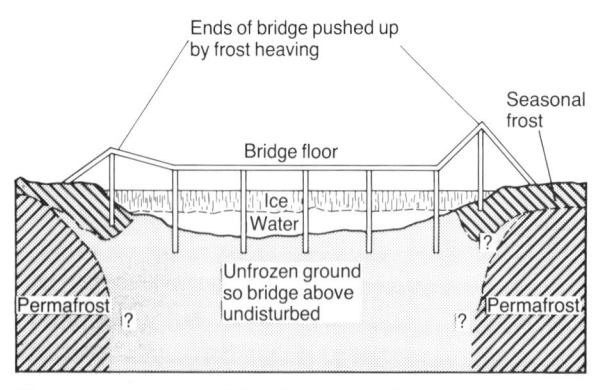

Figure 7 *Damage to a bridge by frost heaving*

In contrast, frost heaving pushed up the steel piles of a bridge. The piles in the river were not affected because the river prevented the ground from freezing (Figure 7).

The bridge and house were both built on fine sands and clays. These hold a lot of water. As a result such soils move a lot when they freeze or thaw.

Building roads

Road building in the Canadian North is very recent. The first roads were built for military use during the Second World War. Others followed, often linking mining settlements with the rest of Canada. But there are still few roads.

Whenever possible the frozen ground is left undisturbed. New roads are built on a layer of gravel covered by a sheet of insulation (Figure 8). These help prevent the permafrost below from thawing.

If cuttings are made or vegetation stripped away then the permafrost is exposed. It thaws and the road subsides or cuttings are buried in a landslide.

Figure 8 *Road building over permafrost*

Building to last

Expensive construction methods are used to keep buildings stable. Low cost buildings are built on gravel pads a metre thick (Figure 9). Gravel drains well so there is less chance of it freezing. But the weight of buildings does cause settling.

Larger buildings rest on timber or concrete piles. The piles pass through the active layer into permanently frozen ground. The holes have to be made by expensive drilling or steaming.

Heat from buildings is a problem. Floors are well-insulated. Clear space of at least half a metre is left under buildings so that cold air can circulate. This keeps the ground frozen (Figure 10).

Figure 9 *Post and pad foundations for homes*

Figure 10 *School on pile foundations*

Pipe problems

Gas, water and sewage pipes can be buried in less cold climates. But pipes in permafrost may fracture because of ground movement. Water will freeze. **Utilidors** are heated tunnel-like boxes which carry the pipes (Figure 11). Above ground they rest on piles or gravel mats.

Exercises

5 Explain what happens to roads, bridges and houses if they are not carefully built. Make a sketch of Figure 6 or 7 to illustrate your answer.

6 Describe how gravel pads, spaces under buildings, piles and utilidors help solve the problem of building on permafrost.

Figure 11 *Utilidors and houses on pile foundations*

4.5 After the ice

When the climate became warmer at the end of a glacial period, the ice began to melt. A new landscape began to emerge as debris from the ice was spread over the land.

Spreading over the land

Soil, sand, gravel and rock debris caught up in the ice is called **moraine**. This moraine is not spread evenly in the ice. Most collects at the side and base because it is in contact with the surrounding rock.

Debris in the base of the ice is called **ground moraine**. It buried East Anglia in a layer 30-40 m thick (Figure 1). In Europe and North America ice sheets left vast plains of this **till** or **boulder clay** (Figure 2).

Figure 1 *A chalk pit with till*

Figure 2 *Boulder clay*

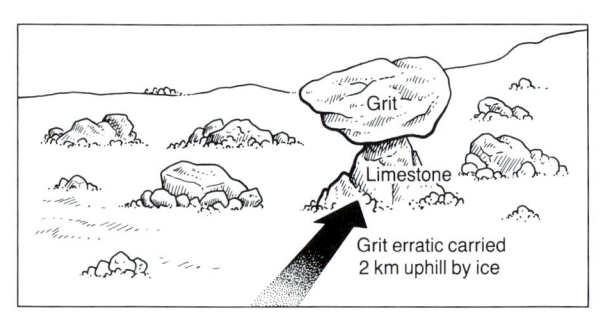

Figure 3 *An erratic*

Signposts of the ice

Some glaciers and ice sheets travelled hundreds of kilometres. Boulders picked up at one place were carried and left in areas of different rock type. Such boulders are called **erratics** (Figure 3).

By finding places made of the same rock type as an erratic, geologists can track down where the ice came from (Figure 4).

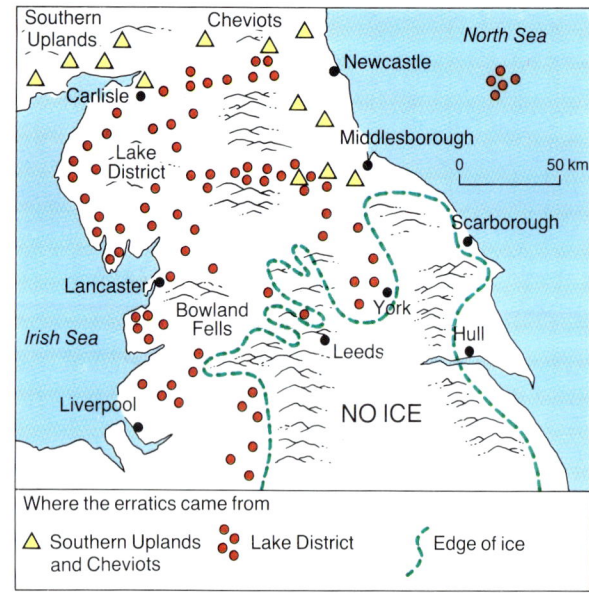

Figure 4 *Erratics in Northern England*

Exercises

1. Why is 'boulder clay' a suitable name for the material in Figure 2?

2. Explain why the rock in Figure 3 is out of place.

3. Make a trace of Figure 4. Draw in arrows to show the directions the ice moved.

Ice continues to move forwards even as it melts. Debris added to end moraine

Previous position of glacier

End moraine fed by debris in ice

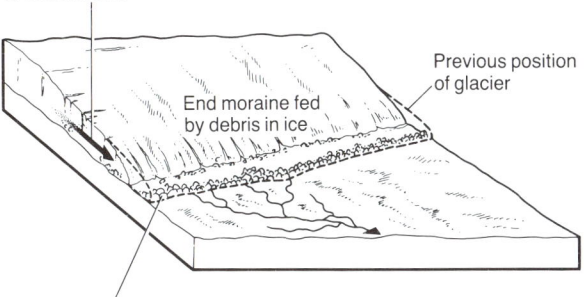

As ice melted at edge so ridge of sand, silt and boulders called an **end moraine** was deposited

Figure 5 *How end moraine was formed*

Pointing the way

The shapes of some moraines show which direction the ice moved. Piles of debris were scraped up and pushed along at the **snout** of a glacier. The snout of a moving valley glacier has a curved shape. This is because the glacier's sides are held back by friction with the valley sides (Figure 5).

When the glacier melts it leaves a curved ridge called an **end** or **terminal moraine**. Its shape shows which way the ice was moving when it began to melt (Figure 6).

Streamlined hills

Rounded hills called **drumlins** are another sign that ice has passed by. They are usually in groups (swarms) and can reach 100 m in height (Figure 7). Drumlins are usually made of boulder clay, though some are carved from solid rock. It is not certain how they are made.

The boulder clay may have been dumped under moving ice. This gave the hills a streamlined shape. Their long axes and gently sloping tails point in the direction of ice movement (Figure 8).

Figure 6 *Jumble of moraines on Eldridge Glacier*

Figure 7 *Drumlins*

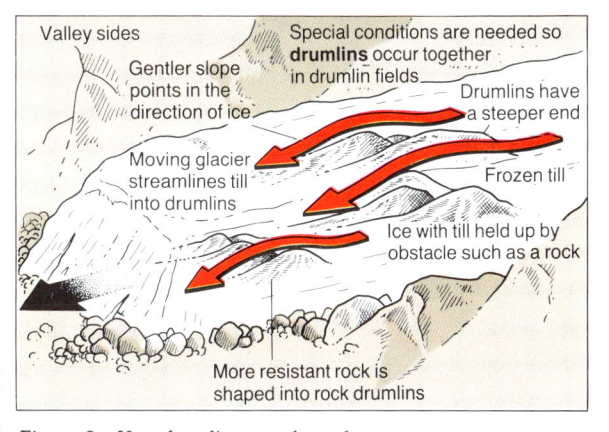

Valley sides
Gentler slope points in the direction of ice
Special conditions are needed so **drumlins** occur together in drumlin fields
Drumlins have a steeper end
Moving glacier streamlines till into drumlins
Frozen till
Ice with till held up by obstacle such as a rock
More resistant rock is shaped into rock drumlins

Figure 8 *How drumlins were formed*

Exercise

4 a Make sketches of Figures 6 and 7.
   b Draw on the direction of ice flow.
   c Add notes to explain how each was formed.

Melting ice

As the Ice Age ended, rising temperatures melted the glaciers and permafrost. Huge volumes of **meltwater** were released. Torrents poured down the valley at Cheddar to deepen and widen it into the present Cheddar Gorge (Figure 9).

An ice sheet dammed up streams against the Cleveland Hills. At first, lakes 50 m deep were formed. Then they spilled over the hills and flowed south in a flood of water (Figure 10). Within twenty years this torrent had carved a valley 250 m wide and up to 100 m deep. Today this **overflow channel** is called Newton Dale (Figure 11).

Figure 9 *Cheddar Gorge*

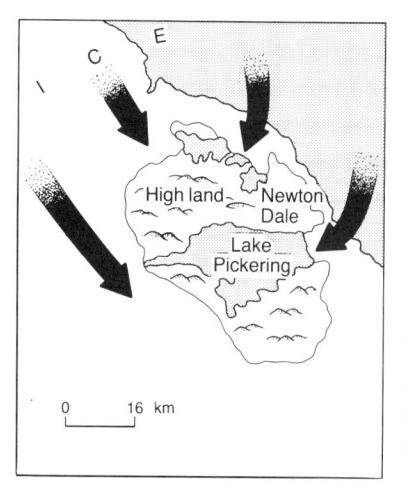

Figure 10 *The Cleveland Hills during the Ice Age*

Figure 11 *Newton Dale overflow channel*

Exercises

5 a What evidence in Figure 9 suggests Cheddar Gorge was made by a river?
  b What suggests that the river was powerful?

6 a Make a sketch of Figure 11.
  b Describe how it was formed. Use Figure 10 to help you.

Figure 12 *An esker in Eire*

Figure 13 *Outwash deposits*

All washed out

Streams flowing under and from the ice are loaded with debris. This is washed from the ice as **outwash deposits**. At the edge or inside the melting ice, streams form winding shaped features called **eskers** (Figure 12).

Outwash in Wisconsin

Ice sheets moved south over Wisconsin in the USA 25 000 years ago (Figure 14). When they began melting, lakes and outwash deposits covered large areas. Some are now fertile farmland, others are forested hills or marshes.

Spreading out

Further from the ice, sands and gravels are spread as **outwash fans** and **plains**. Debris left by rivers of melted ice is called **fluvioglacial** deposits. They are well sorted by the streams. Larger gravel is deposited nearest the ice. Finer material such as sand is carried further away (Figure 13).

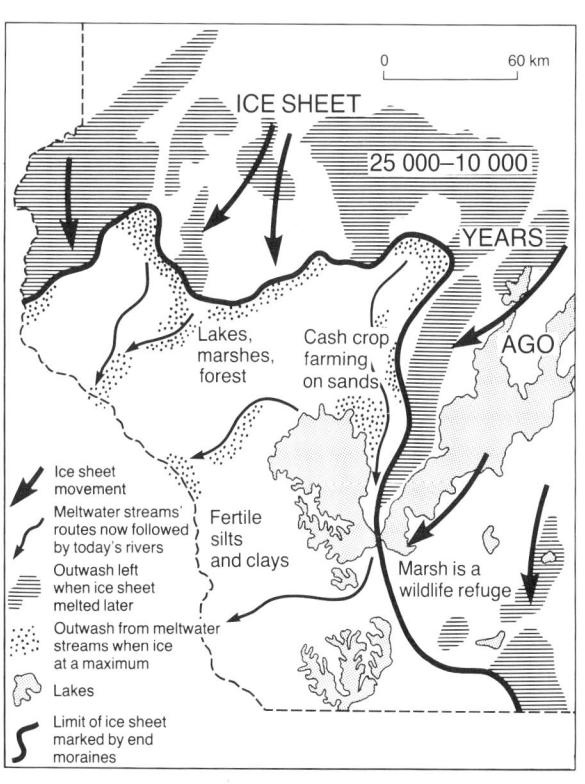

Figure 14 *Outwash in Wisconsin*

Exercises

7 Study Figure 12
 a Describe an esker.
 b Contrast the way people have used the eskers and the surrounding land.

8 a What are fluvioglacial deposits?
 b Why are larger gravels found nearer the melting glacier and finer sands and clays further away?

9 a Use the scale on Figure 14 to show that meltwater streams affected large areas.
 b Describe the different ways people use fluvioglacial deposits in Wisconsin.

Changing sea levels

The peak of the last glacial period was 20 000 years ago. At that time, world sea levels were 120 m below the present level. Much of the world's water was locked up as ice. As the ice melted, sea levels rose and land near the coast was flooded.

Flooding the land

Large inlets were made where valleys reached the sea. Their shape and depth depended on the relief of the land. Deep V-shaped valleys on highland coasts became **rias** (Figure 15).

There are many examples of rias around the coasts of south west England and Ireland. The deep sheltered water is used as harbours for all types of shipping. The ria at Salcombe in Devon is a smaller, more shallow example (Figure 16).

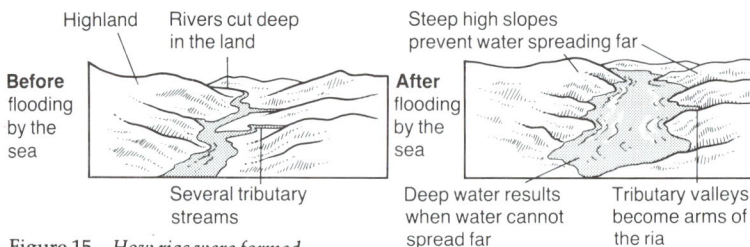

Figure 15 How rias were formed

Inlets and estuaries

Along low-lying coasts, the rising sea could flood valleys and spread out over the land. Shallow inlets a few metres deep were formed (Figure 17). There are many examples of these **estuaries** in eastern England.

Figure 16 The ria at Salcombe in Devon

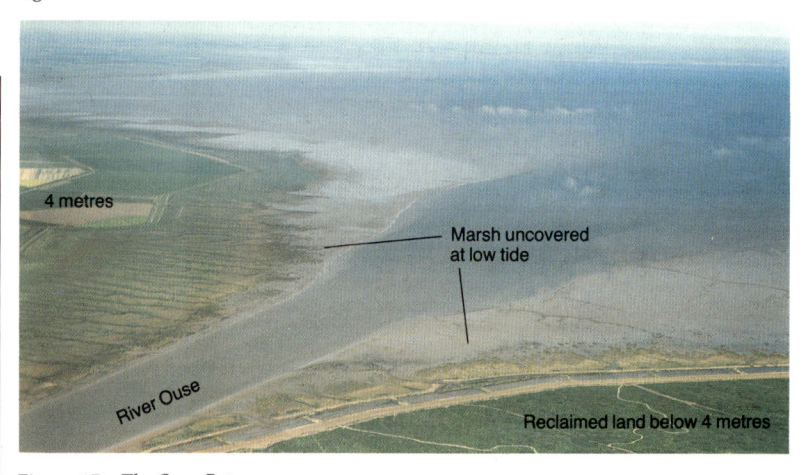

Figure 17 The Ouse Estuary

Exercises

10 a Make a sketch of Figure 16.
   b Label on: depths ... arms ... height of surrounding hilltops ... high tide mark.

11 a Use Figure 17 to compare a ria and an estuary.
   b Why are they different?

Figure 18 *Sogne Fiord*

The fiord coast

Glaciated valleys were drowned to form the **fiords** of western Norway (Figure 18) and the coastal lochs of western Scotland. Some glaciers over 300 m thick and more than a kilometre wide, carved very deep valleys. This meant that the rising sea could flood far inland to great depths.

Sogne Fiord in Norway is 204 km long and up to 1303 m deep (Figure 19). Glaciers also deepened its tributary valleys so the fiord has many branches.

Exercises

12 Draw or trace a map of the coast of north west Scotland or western Norway. Name the main lochs or fiords.

13 Why are fiords so much deeper and longer than rias or estuaries?

14 Make a labelled sketch of Figure 18. Use Figure 19 to help you.

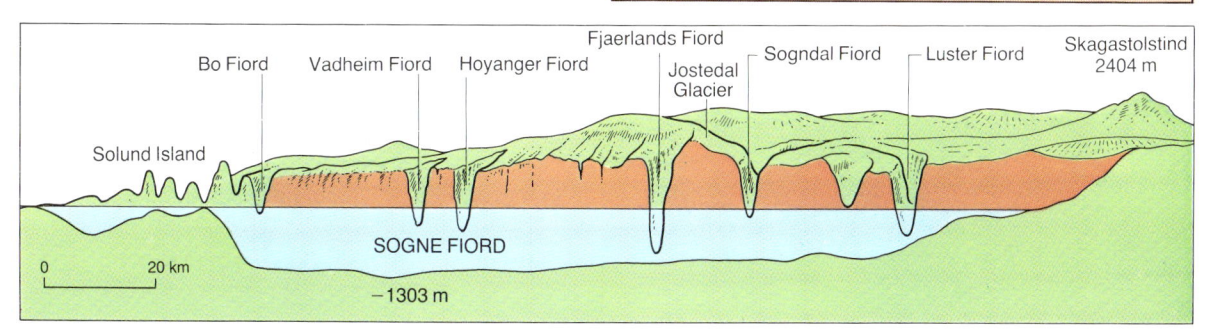

Figure 19 *Cross-section of the Sogne Fiord*

Going up

Fiords, rias and estuaries were formed by the widespread change in sea level. This is called **eustatic** change.

In some places, the level of the land has changed. This is called **isostatic** change. During the glacial periods, the huge weight of ice pushed the crust down. An ice sheet 300 m thick can depress the crust by 100 m. When the ice melted, the crust rose again and the land was uplifted (Figure 20).

Figure 20 *Glacial uplift in Scotland*

High and dry

Beaches formed during the Ice Age have been raised above the present sea level. Behind these **raised beaches** are fossil cliffs (Figure 21). The raised beaches are the top of present-day cliffs. Bands of sand and pebbles mark their position in the cliff face (Figure 22).

Figure 21 *Raised beach in Western Scotland*

Exercises

15 Study Figure 20.
  a Which parts of Scotland have risen most?
  b Give a reason for this. (Hint: thickness of the ice.)

16 a Make a sketch of Figure 21.
  b Label on: 10 m raised beach ... old cliff ... present beach ... ways people have used the raised beach ... wave-cut platform.
  c Explain how the beach was formed. Use Figure 20 to help you.

17 Study Figure 22.
  What evidence is there for a raised beach?

Figure 22 *Profile of a raised beach*

UNIT 5 The desert scene

5.1 Introduction

Most people picture a desert as a landscape of sand and oases. In fact, only 30 per cent of desert land is like this. Most is stony and rocky.

Desert landscapes

Stones and rocks are the most common type of desert surface. The desert plains are often littered with both rounded and sharp-edged stones (Figure 1). These rest on a layer of sand, silt or clay a few centimetres thick. In some places, a bare rock pavement is exposed. This bare rock is called a **reg** in North Africa and a **gibber plain** in Australia.

There are also hills and even mountains in some deserts. The larger deserts have a variety of desert landscapes (Figure 2).

A special environment

There is little rainfall in desert areas so there is little plant growth. Areas like this, with under 250 mm of rainfall each year are said to be **arid**.

Deserts are difficult places for people to live in, not only because of the scarcity of water. High daytime temperatures of over 37°C and a fall of 20°C at night are common.

In such a climate, the effects of weathering and erosion are different from those in humid countries such as the UK (Figure 3).

Figure 1 *Stony desert*

Figure 2 *A desert landscape*

Figure 3 *Desert features*

Exercises

1 In what ways is Figure 1 typical of a desert?

2 Use Figure 2 to draw an imaginary desert landscape.

3 Study Figure 3.
   Describe how you think desert erosion and weathering will be different from that in the UK.

5.2 Breaking the desert rocks

Desert sand, stones and boulders are made by weathering. Some lie as screes where they have broken off. Others are moved away by wind, rainwash and even rivers.

Hot and cold

Large daily temperature changes cause **mechanical weathering** in deserts. During the day, the bare rock is baked and the surface expands. At night, temperatures fall steeply and the rock cools down.

This **high diurnal range** of temperaure causes enough stress in the rock for pieces to break off. This process is called **insolation weathering**.

Joints are widened and more rock becomes exposed to the heating and cooling. Minerals in a rock expand and contract by different amounts (Figure 1). For instance the darker minerals usually expand the most. The weakest mineral crumbles first then the rest fall apart.

Figure 1 *The minerals in igneous rock*

Frequent fogs

The Namib and Atacama deserts have around 200 days with fog each year (Figure 2). About 40 mm of moisture is deposited annually out of the fog. This moisture can chill hot rock and act as a type of insolation weathering.

Exercises

1. a How do temperature changes break up rock?
   b What is this process called?

2. a How do fogs help weather rock?
   b Name the deserts where this often happens (Figure 2).

Figure 2 *Desert fog*

Figure 3 *Salt weathering*

Salt weathering

High temperaures also cause **salt weathering** (Figure 3). Salts from ground water, rain or dew are left behind when moisture is evaporated. They fill and expand the rock's pore spaces and help break up the rock.

Some salt crystals expand by taking up moisture. This expansion causes more stress and more weathering.

Desert frosts

In hot deserts, temperatures in the high land can fall to below 0°C at night. In cold deserts, such as the Gobi, winters are severe. Rock is shattered by frost and ice (Figure 4).

Figure 4 *Frost shattering*

Exercises

3 a Make a sketch of Figure 5.
   b Label on the various ways the rock could have been weathered.

4 Deserts are often said to be 'dry and hot'. From what you have learned, explain how desert weathering shows that this is not completely true.

Figure 5 *Desert cliffs*

5.3 Desert water

Many landforms in deserts are made by running water. This may seem odd where there may be no rainfall and no rivers for year after year.

Flash floods

Running water is very effective when it does flow. The type of rainfall and the lack of vegetation are important reasons for this.

Some rain comes in storms of great intensity. In Rawlinna in Western Australia, 100 mm fell in one day. An average UK rainy day brings 4 mm. Rawlinna's annual rainfall is only 186 mm! Raging torrents called **flash floods** develop quickly and sweep all before them (Figure 1).

Gullies and badlands

Streams become swollen after most rains. The rain runs off quickly where there are bare rock surfaces. There is not enough vegetation, soil and weathered rock to absorb the rain.

The run-off can carve deep gashes called **gullies** down slopes, across roads and through fields (Figure 2). In the USA gullies are a feature of the **Badlands**.

Figure 1 *Flash flood*

Rivers as carriers

Desert streams are usually short-lived. Water either evaporates away or sinks into the ground as **percolation**. As they shrink in volume and energy, they deposit their loads. Channels become choked with debris.

Rivers transport weathered rock across the land (Figure 3). With little vegetation to anchor them, sand and stones are swept into streams by the wind and rain.

Valleys in the desert

Desert valleys that are usually dry are called **wadis**. They vary in size and shape. On flat or gently sloping land, they are no more than dried-up river beds (Figure 4). In the mountains, they are deep gorges (Figure 5).

Figure 2 *Badland gulleying in Dakota*

Figure 3　*River braiding in Arizona*

Figure 4　*A shallow wadi*

Rivers in the past

The number and depth of wadi valleys is surprising (Figure 6). Some form a network which could not have been made by today's rainfall and streams. They may have formed when the climate was wetter and rivers flowed all year round. Such **pluvial periods** occured during warmer periods of the Ice Age.

Figure 5　*A wadi as a deep gorge in Morocco*

Exercises

1. a What are flash floods?
   b What is surprising about having floods in deserts
   c Why do they happen?

2. a Why are desert streams often short-lived?
   b How do their channels become choked with debris?

3. Imagine you are on a desert expedition. You want to find evidence to show desert areas were wetter in the past.
   What evidence would you look for? Use Figures 4, 5 and 6 to help you. Illustrate your answer with a map and sketch.

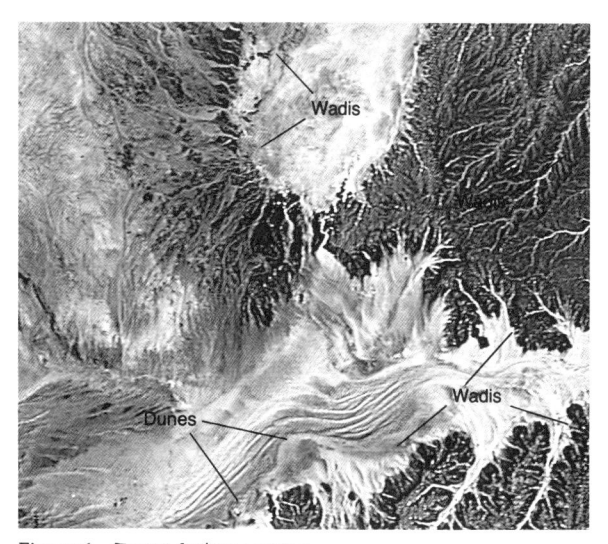

Figure 6　*Desert drainage system*

Problem plains

Around the edges of desert uplands are plains carved into solid rock. These are called **pediments** (Figure 7). The way they are formed is still a puzzle.

The weathering back of the uplands may be one explanation. The upland slopes wear back parallel to each other (Figure 8). The weathered rock is carried away by surface wash and streams.

Figure 7 *Pediment, In Salah, in Algeria*

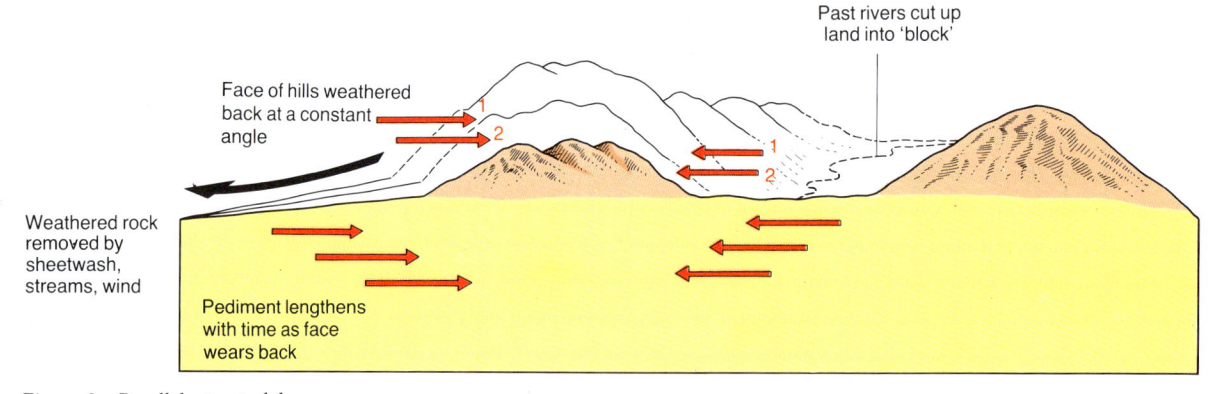

Figure 8 *Parallel retreat of slopes*

Isolated hills

The pediments meet the uplands at a sharp angle. In time the uplands will be worn back by gullying and weathering until an **inselberg** remains (Figure 9).

Exercise

4 Make labelled sketches of Figure 7 and Figure 9. Add notes to explain how they were formed.

Figure 9 *Inselbergs and desert plains in Namibia*

Salts at the surface

Hard layers rich in salts are formed at or below the desert surface. This **desert crust** is usually less than a metre thick. In some places the salts cement sand, gravels or clay together to make a very hard crust called a **hardpan**. This hardpan can be over 40 m thick.

The high evaporation and low rainfall in deserts cause these salt-rich layers (Figure 10). In wetter climates, the salts would have been washed down through the soil.

Figure 10 *A white fringe of salts around an evaporating lake*

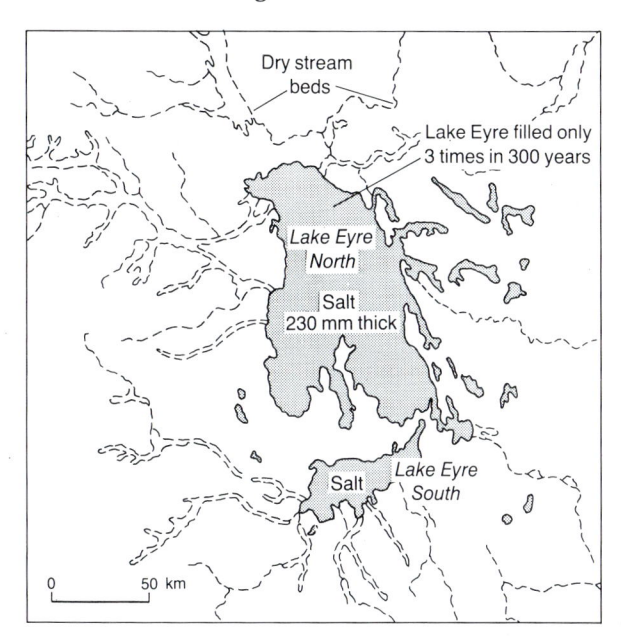

Figure 11 *Lake Eyre: an inland drainage basin*

Figure 12 *A creek entering Lake Eyre*

Salt lakes

After intense rainfall or flooding, desert hollows may fill with lakes. Some, such as Lake Eyre in Australia and Lake Chad in Africa, are huge centres of **inland drainage** (Figure 11).

Even the largest lakes evaporate and shrink in size. They leave a crust of clays and salt which cracks as it dries out (Figure 12).

Exercises

5 Imagine you are writing a report about a newly-discovered area of desert crust. Say what its possibilities are for:
   a farming
   b new roads
   c flooding

6 Find a map of Lake Chad in your atlas. Draw a similar map to that in Figure 11.

5.4 Water for people

Some countries are mostly desert. It is often difficult and expensive to find enough water for all the people. New ways of getting water have to be found.

Arid Bahrain

The state of Bahrain is small. It has only 400 000 people and its thirteen islands cover just 607 km² (Figure 1). The climate is hot and humid. In August the average temperature reaches 34°C and falls to 16.8°C on average in January. The rainfall of 72.5 mm a year is low and erratic. In 1946 it was as low as 1.6 mm but 168.9 mm fell in 1959! Such rainfall is too small to support the people of Bahrain. They have to look elsewhere for their water supplies.

Water from underground

For 5000 years the people have collected water from springs and wells. They water their crops with it. Water from underground is called **ground water**. Very little of this water comes from rain falling on Bahrain.

Most is from parts of Saudi Arabia 250 kilometres to the west (Figure 2). The water flows through permeable rock which dips towards Bahrain. Rocks storing water underground are **aquifers**. Bahrain's aquifer water is thousands of years old. It began as rain on Saudi Arabia when the climate was much wetter than today.

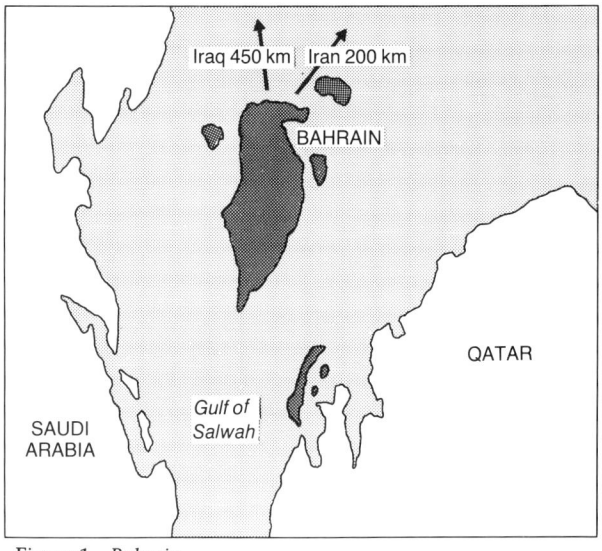

Figure 1 *Bahrain*

Exercises

1 Explain why people in Bahrain have had to use ground water.

2 a What is an aquifer?
   b Make a sketch of Figure 2.
   c Explain how ground water gets into a well in Bahrain.
   d Why is the water so old?

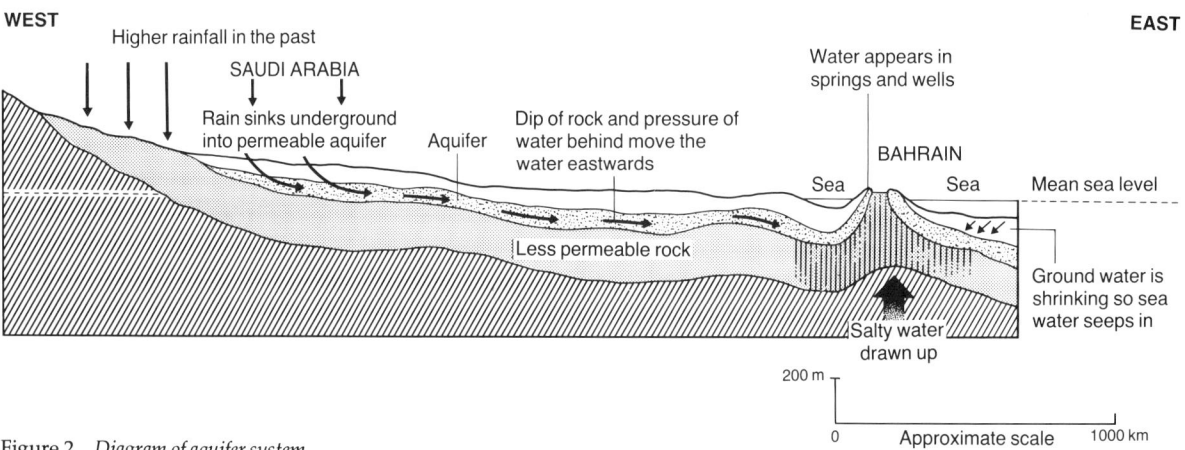

Figure 2 *Diagram of aquifer system*

Shrinking supplies

The demand for water is increasing. Since 1925 a thousand boreholes have been drilled. Until 1960 there was a dramatic increase in water taken from underground (Figure 3). Once used the water takes hundreds of years to replace.

Too much ground water has been taken. The level underground has fallen 4.5 m. Sea water and deep-lying salts are contaminating supplies. Springs have dried up.

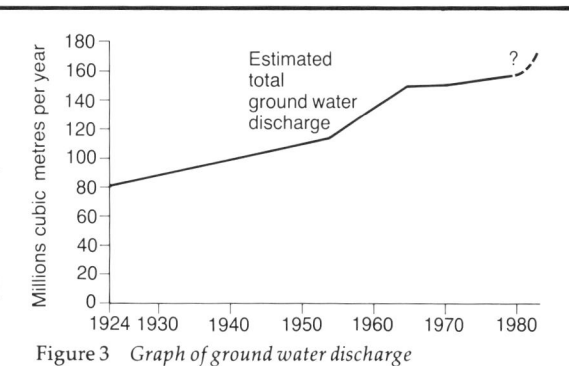

Figure 3   Graph of ground water discharge

A salty solution

The government of Bahrain is using sea water to solve its water supply problem. **Desalination plants** have been built which purify the sea water (Figure 4). By 1986 the bulk of Bahrain's water supply came from these plants. The government also wants people to use less water in their homes. People are charged for the amount of water they use. This may make them use less.

Figure 4   A desalination plant

Exercises

3 What do the following figures tell you?

Ground water used per year	1925 83 million m^3	1985 170 million m^3
Sources of water supply	1984 45 400m^3 a day from aquifers 22 700m^3 a day from desalination plants	1986 81 800m^3 a day from aquifers 150 000m^3 a day from desalination plants

4 What two problems result from taking too much ground water?

5 How is the government of Bahrain trying to solve their water supply problem?

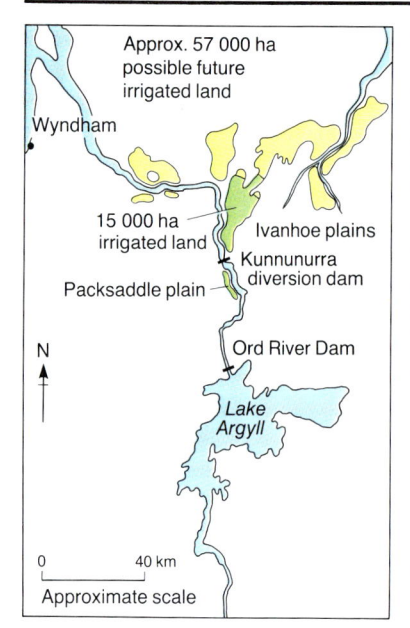

Figure 6 Map of Ord River irrigation project

Figure 7 The Ord River area
(a) before irrigation
(b) after irrigation

	Jan	Feb	Mar	Apr	May	Jun	Jul	Aug	Sep	Oct	Nov	Dec	Year
Wyndham (tropical monsoon)													
Mean max. temp. °C	36.2	35.7	35.8	35.4	32.9	30.3	30.2	32.2	34.9	36.9	37.7	37.1	34.6
Rainfall mm	146	214	214	29	15	8	1	0	12	19	57	95	769
Rawlinna (desert)													
Mean max. temp. °C	32.9	31.7	29.6	25.5	21.7	18.6	17.9	19.8	23.4	26.3	29.6	31.7	25.7
Rainfall mm	14	17	18	18	17	19	14	16	13	14	13	13	186

Figure 5 Climatic statistics for Wyndham and Rawlinna

Water for crops

Crops can be grown in deserts if enough water is available. The north of Western Australia is not a desert, but it has a tropical monsoon climate with a marked dry season between April and September (Figure 5). Temperatures are as high as those in a desert.

The Ord River Irrigation Project

The Ord River has been dammed. The reservoirs behind the dams provide water to **irrigate** crops (Figure 6). Land which was low quality cattle grazing has become productive cropland (Figure 7).

The Ord River Dam controls the flow of the river. During the wet season the river is a raging torrent. The dam stores up the water in Lake Argyll so it is available to farmers throughout the year. Fifty kilometres downstream the Kununurra Diversion Dam diverts the water to the farms.

Exercises

6   Study the climatic figures in Figure 5.
    a Describe the ways Wyndham's climate is similar to Rawlinna's desert climate.
    b Why do crops need irrigation in the Wyndham area?

7   Study Figure 6.
    a How much land is irrigated now?
    b How much could be irrigated in the future?
    c Name a future use of the Ord River Dam. Why is the dam not used for this at the moment?

Laying out the land

Irrigation schemes have to be carefully engineered. For instance Lake Kununurra stands higher than the farms. Its water can reach them under gravity. Farm fields are **graded** so the irrigation water spreads evenly (Figure 8). But the land has to slope enough for water to drain away. Salts will be left if water is allowed to stand and evaporate. The soil will become less fertile.

Starting from scratch

Before the Ord River Project was given the go-ahead, crop trials took place for twelve years. It was not known if crops could be successfully grown in the area. The Kimberley Research Station found that several crops grew well (Figure 9) so the land was opened up to farmers.

Counting the cost

Irrigation projects are expensive. The Ord River Project has cost over $A30 million. But there are many benefits. Crops grow where none could before (Figure 7). Although the soils are heavy clays they give good **yields**. **Intensive farming** is possible. Seeds can be closely planted and the soil well fertilized.

Because crops can be grown all year, **double cropping** is possible. For example rice is grown during the wet season followed by irrigated maize in the same field during the dry season.

Figure 10 *Ord River irrigation area*

Figure 8 *An irrigated crop*

A number of crops have been investigated at Kimberley Research Station.

Bananas*	Guar	Pineapples
Basil	Kenal	Rapeseed
Barley	Lablab	Rice*
Castorbean	Lemon grass	Safflower
Chickpeas	Lime	Sesame
Cowpeas	Linseed	Sorghum*
Cucurbits*	Millet*	Soy beans*
Citrus – lemon,	Maize*	Sugar cane*
grapefruit,	Mangoes*	Sunflower*
mandarin	Niger	Sweet potatoes
Cotton	Oats*	Tobacco
Coriander	Peanuts*	Triticale
Cassava		Wheat*

* Crops grown on farms
The other crops are not grown commercially at this stage as yields and returns are too low

Figure 9 *Crops investigated at Kimberley Research Station*

Exercise

8 You are asked to make a study of an imaginary arid area. Like the Ord River area, it has a dry season and a river runs through it. You have to draw up a plan to develop the area for irrigated crop farming.
   a Describe your plan. Mention: choosing the right crops ... controlling the river ... grading the land ... finance
   b Use Figure 7 to describe how the landscape would change.
   c Describe the advantages you would expect from irrigated cropping.

5.5 Sands of time

Early travellers from Europe wondered at the vastness of desert sands. The sands of the Rub al Khali in Saudi Arabia cover 560 000 km². This is an area bigger than France!

Sand on the move

Wind-blown sand is called **aeolian sand**. Fine, dust-like grains are lifted in **suspension** as in dust storms. Most larger grained sand moves with a jumping action called **saltation**. The sand becomes heaped into sand dunes. In Oman, the Wahiba Sands cover an area of 9500 km² (Figure 1).

Across the wind

Different wind flows and varying amounts of sand cause a variety of dunes in Wahiba. In the south and east, the dominant wind comes from the south west. There is a plentiful supply of sand. Closely spaced dunes have developed across the path of the wind. They are **transverse dunes** (Figure 2). Where the sand supply is more limited then the crescent-shaped **barchans** are formed (Figures 3 and 4). Barchans are not widespread in deserts.

The dunes make regular patterns. For instance, the transverse dunes are 10 m high and 200-300 m apart. This pattern probably results from the regular flow of winds.

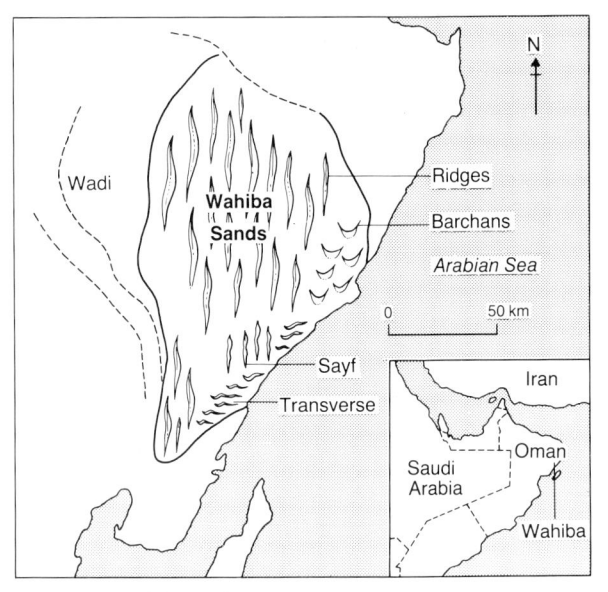

Figure 1 *Wahiba sands*

Figure 2 *Transverse dunes*

Figure 3 *Barchans*

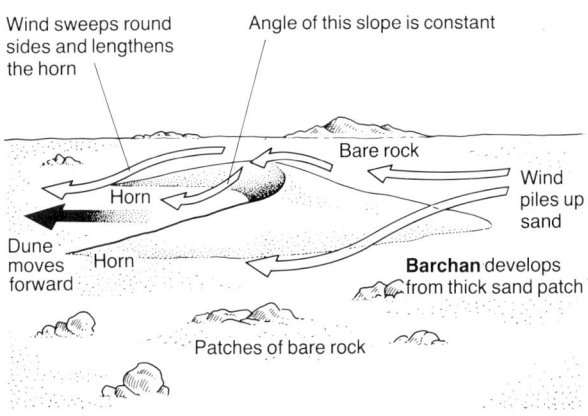

Figure 4 *How barchans are formed*

Ridges of sand

The **Sayf** dune is an example of how wind conditions affect the shape of dunes. Sayfs are winding ridges which run parallel to the main winds (Figure 5). They are formed from transverse dunes. These are broken up and 'stretched' by easterly winds (Figure 6).

Figure 5 *Sayf dunes*

Whirling air

The backbone of the Wahiba Sands is made up of 100 m high ridges running north to south (Figure 7). The hot desert surface and the roughness of sand patches causes winds to eddy. This whirling of the air is called **helical air-flow** (Figure 8). The eddies sweep the sand into ridges separated by depressions called **swales**. Active dunes rest on the ridges.

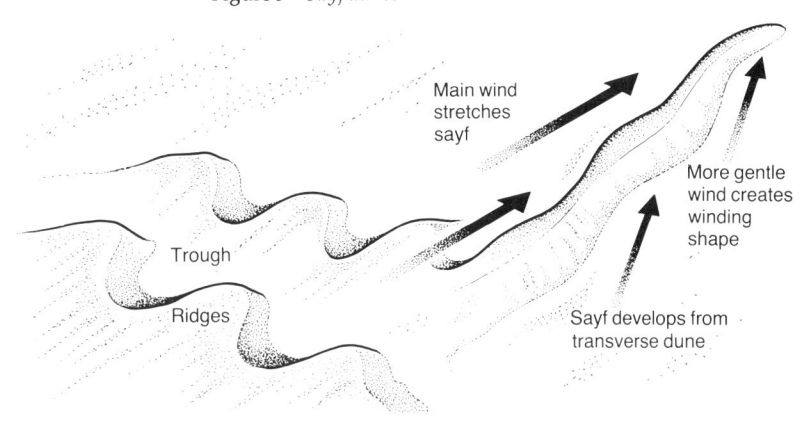

Figure 6 *The formation of sayf dunes*

Figure 7 *Mega ridges*

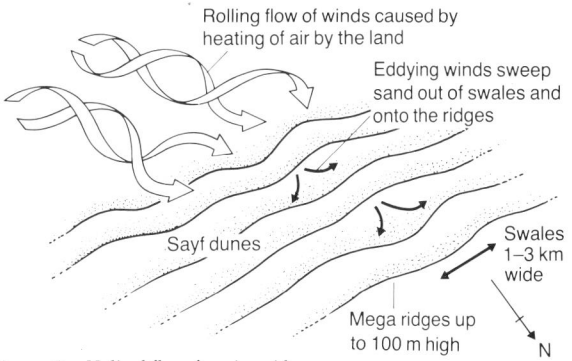

Figure 8 *Helical flow forming ridges*

Exercises

1 Draw a diagram to show how sand moves.

2 Match the correct dune to each of these descriptions.
   long ridges parallel to the wind
   ridges across the line of wind direction
   made by reshaping transverse dunes
   shaped by helical air-flow
   heaped up from patches of sand

3 Draw two labelled sketches to show dunes:
   a mostly shaped from another type of dune
   b requiring special wind conditions

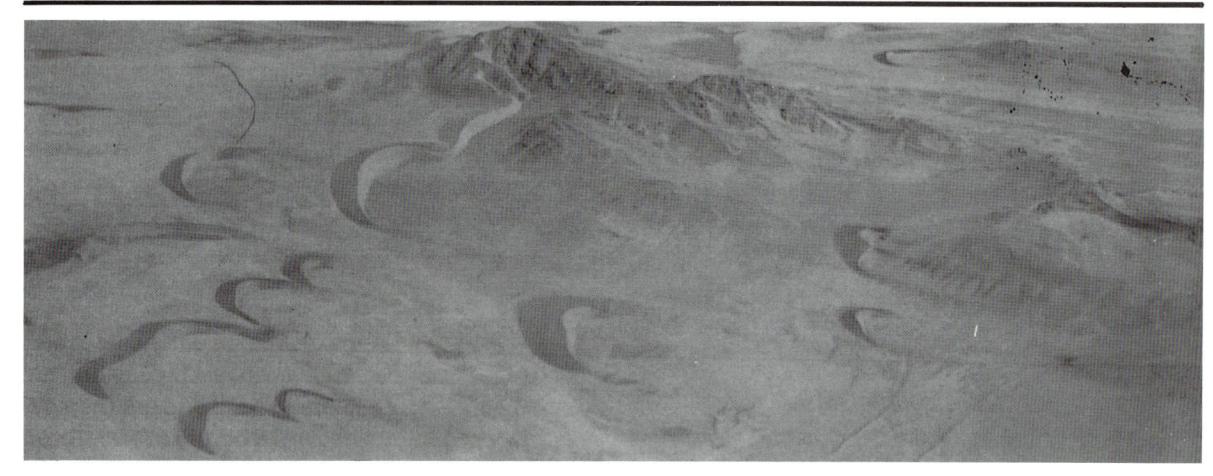

Figure 9 Wind-streamlined rocks

Scoured by the wind

Wind erosion is not so important as water and weathering in shaping deserts. In some deserts, however, features shaped by wind erosion are common.

In the Tibesti region of the Sahara deep grooves 100 m deep and many kilometres long cover an area of 90 000 km^2. They are carved in solid rock. Satellite photos show them stretched out in the direction of the main winds (Figure 9).

Blasted by sand

Sand grains are commonly made of quartz. When blown against rock the hard grains have a **sandblasting** effect. Usually the wind only lifts grains 50-60 cm from the ground. Rock above this is less wind eroded. Occasionally rocks are rounded and streamlined into **yardangs** (Figure 10). These features are not common.

Figure 10 Yardangs

Exercises

4 a Describe the feature shown on Figure 9. Use the text to help you.
   b What evidence is there that it was formed by wind erosion?

5 a Make a sketch of Figure 10.
   b Label it with these words: streamlining by wind ... rounding by sandblasting ... height _____ metres.

Grooved and polished

Smoothing and polishing by the wind is widespread (Figure 11). It is too fine to be done by sandblasting. The wind itself, sometimes with dust, does the work.

In the Namib desert this **wind blast** forms mostly small scale features. Rocks have grooves under 2 m long and 1-10 m deep. This is called **fluting** (Figure 12). The wind can pick out weaker areas in a rock and **etch** them into different shapes (Figure 13).

Figure 11 Rock smoothing

Figure 12 Fluting

Figure 13 Etching

Wind deflation

There is another way by which the wind erodes. It scours out hollows by blowing the sand away (Figure 14). This is called **wind deflation**. Such desert depressions are common and are often streamlined in the direction of the winds. The number and size of sand and dust storms shows the vast quantities of sand moved by deflation.

Figure 14 Deflation hollows

Exercises

6 a In which continent and country is the Namib Desert?
  b Describe the features made by wind blasting in the Namib Desert.
  c Why is wind blast rather than sandblasting a more likely explanation for these?

7 a What is wind deflation?
  b Give two pieces of evidence to suggest that some hollows are made by the wind.

107

Figure 15 Al-Hasa Oasis, Saudi Arabia

Figure 16 Oasis crops

Figure 17 Palm tree overwhelmed by sand

Figure 18 Tamarisk trees

Oasis under threat

Sometimes the moving sand threatens the way of life of desert people. For 2000 years the Al-Hasa Oasis in Saudi Arabia has been under attack from sand dunes (Figure 15).

The main crops grown are rice and dates (Figure 16). Homes, fields and palm trees have disappeared under the sand. Some become uncovered again. Half the oasis has disappeared in the past 1000 years.

Overwhelmed by sand

Northerly winds blowing between April and June move the dunes an average of 4.5 m a year. Sand begins moving when wind speeds are 5.5 metres per second (m/s) but winds of 7.5 m/s are most effective. Storms winds are not frequent but they shift vast amounts of sand. Even large palm trees are overwhelmed (Figure 17).

Stopping the sand

In 1962 the Saudi Government started a sand stabilization project. Fences have been built to stop the dunes. But planting local Tamarisk trees is the main defence (Figure 18).

The project has not been completely successful. The oasis is still in danger.

Exercise

8 Write a newspaper report about the Al-Hasa Oasis. Mention:
   the shifting sand dunes ... the damage they are doing ... what is being done to solve the problems.
   Give your report a striking headline!

UNIT 6   Landscapes in change

6.1   Introduction

Each year the Yellow River in China carries 1600 million tonnes of sediment to the sea. This mud, sand and gravel has been removed from the land by weathering and erosion.

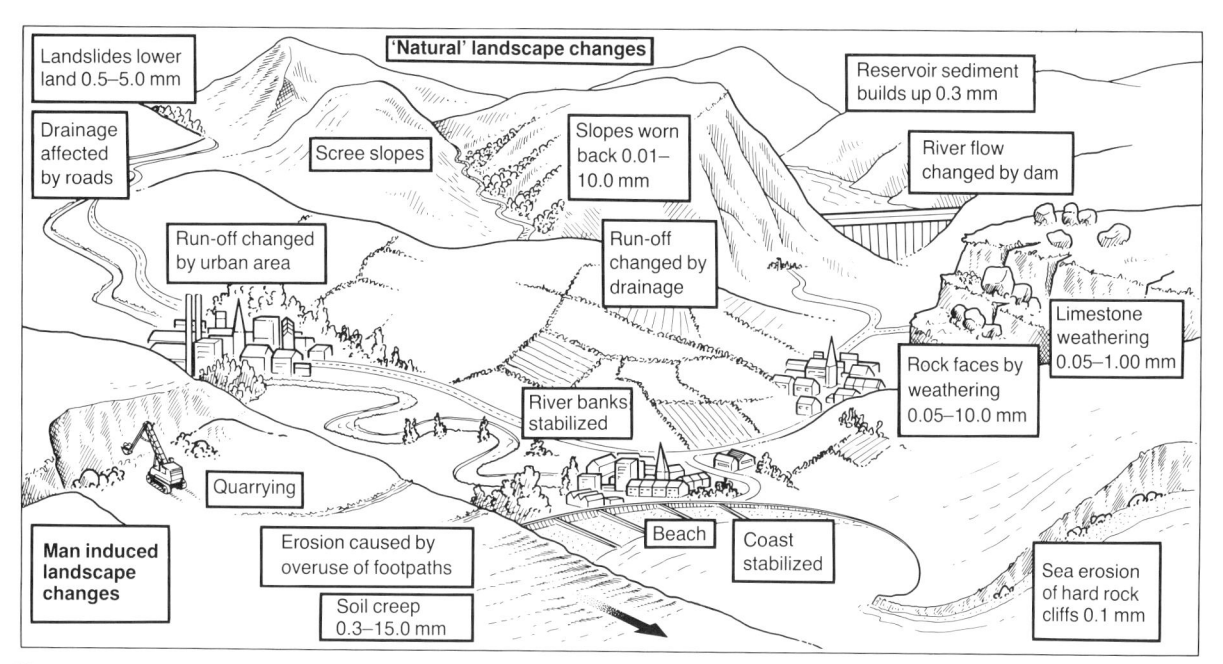

Figure 1 *An imaginary British landscape*

Labels on figure:
- 'Natural' landscape changes
- Landslides lower land 0.5–5.0 mm
- Drainage affected by roads
- Scree slopes
- Slopes worn back 0.01–10.0 mm
- Reservoir sediment builds up 0.3 mm
- River flow changed by dam
- Run-off changed by urban area
- Run-off changed by drainage
- Limestone weathering 0.05–1.00 mm
- Rock faces by weathering 0.05–10.0 mm
- River banks stabilized
- Quarrying
- Man induced landscape changes
- Erosion caused by overuse of footpaths
- Beach
- Coast stabilized
- Sea erosion of hard rock cliffs 0.1 mm
- Soil creep 0.3–15.0 mm

The time it takes

The speed at which this **denudation** takes place varies from place to place. It is rapid under wet tropical climates. It is much slower where rocks are hard. Over millions of years, land can be levelled by denudation processes. Figure 1 is a sketch of an imaginary British landscape. It shows some of the denudation processes at work.

The hand of 'man'

During the 20th century the work of people has speeded up rates of denudation. People have tunnelled, quarried and cut their way into the land. In Papua New Guinea forests have been cut down. Ground loss measured in mm/1000 years has increased 7.5 times in the past 20 years.

Exercises

1 Study Figure 1.
   a Make a list of the natural denudation processes.
   b Name three things which influence the rate at which denudation takes place.
   c Make a list of the ways people help wear away the land.

2 Describe the ways people and nature wear away the land in your local area (describe things you have actually seen).

6.2 Volcanic landscapes

Iceland is coming apart at the seams! It is one of the world's most active volcanic areas where almost every type of volcanic feature is found.

Heading west

The North American plate began to move west from the European plate about 30 million years ago. The mid-Atlantic ridge marks the present plate boundaries (Figure 1). Iceland lies on this ridge.

As the plates pull apart, molten rock comes to the surface to make new crust. Most of Iceland is made from this material (Figure 2). The rocks are mostly younger than 16 million years old with 10 per cent less than 10 000 years old.

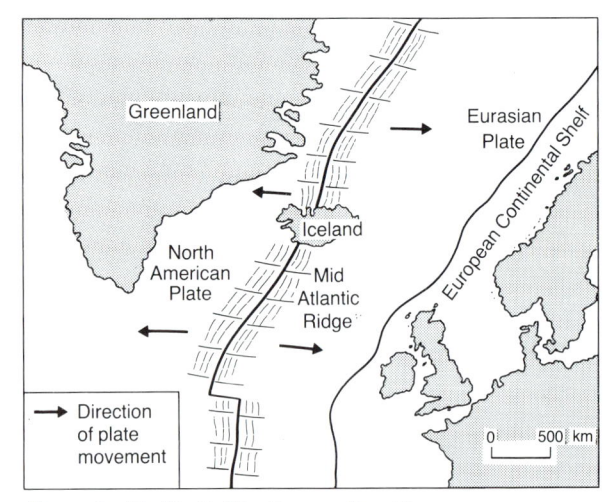

Figure 1 *The North Atlantic spreading ridge*

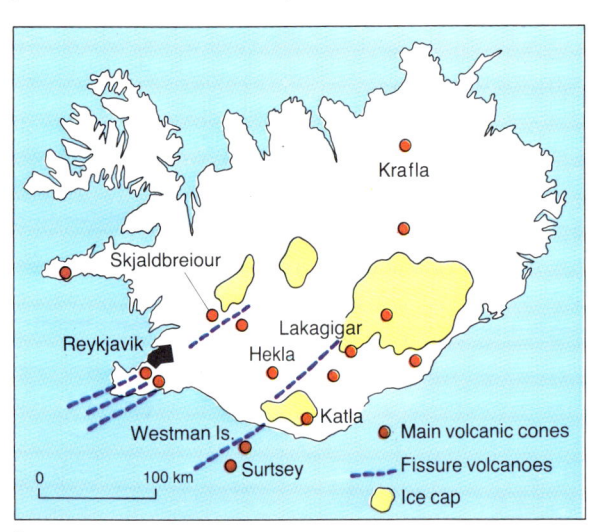

Figure 2 *Iceland geology*

Figure 3 *A fissure eruption near the Krafla crater*

Fountains of fire

There is one volcanic eruption in Iceland about every five years. The most common type is a **fissure eruption**. This is where lava flows from a crack that can be several kilometres long.

In 1981, an 8 km long fissure opened up near the Krafla crater (Figure 3). A sheet of erupting lava made a spectacular fountain of fire.

Sometimes the lava flows from a series of craters along a fissure. The Lakagigar fissure is 30 km long with about 100 craters.

Exercises

1. Use Figure 1 to explain these things:
   a. Why there are active volcanoes on Iceland
   b. Why rocks on Iceland are young

2. a. Explain what is meant by a fissure eruption.
   b. Draw a sketch of Figure 3. Label it to show:
      where it happened
      what kind of eruption it was
      dimensions of the eruption

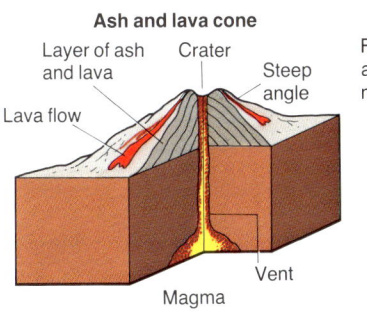

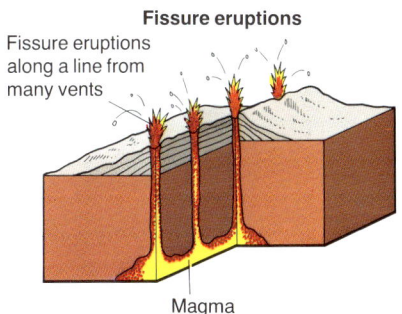

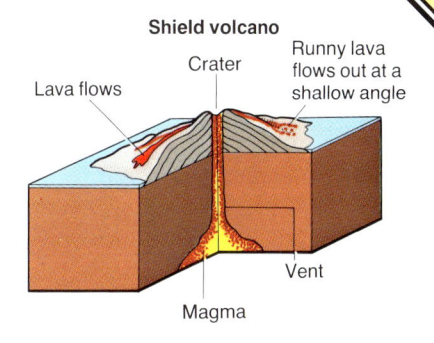

Figure 4 *Types of volcano*

Building cones

About 200 volcanoes have erupted in Iceland over the last 10 000 years. Most types of eruption have taken place at some time (Figure 4).

Lava cones are built when lava erupts through a narrow central **vent** and flows out from the crater. Snaefellsjokull at 1446 m is one of these.

Some cones have very steep sides. These are built up of **acid lava** which does not flow far.

Volcanoes which are still likely to erupt are called **active**. A **dormant** volcano has not erupted for thousands of years. An **extinct** volcano is one that will never erupt again.

Melting the ice

Many of Iceland's volcanoes are under ice. When they erupt, the ice melts and there is widespread flooding. Fortunately this does not happen often.

Shield volcanoes

Some of the older volcanoes are **shield** volcanoes such as at Skjaldbreiur. These slope at a shallow angle. This is caused by runny **basic lava** spreading out over a large area. Hekla is an active shield volcano still capable of violent eruptions and lava flows, though most are from small new craters on the volcano's outer and inner slopes (Figure 5).

Exercises

3 Copy the diagrams which show different kinds of volcano (Figure 4).

4 List and explain the three terms used to show how often a volcano is likely to erupt.

5 a Explain why some volcanic cones have steep slopes, and others have gentle slopes.
   b Describe what is happening in Figure 5.

6 a What special problem is caused in Iceland when some volcanoes erupt? (Hint: ice.)
   b Name one volcano that is under ice. Look back to Figure 2.

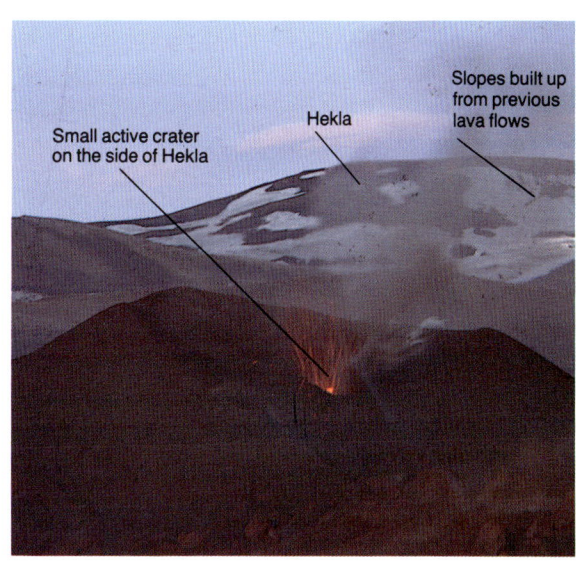

Figure 5 *A new active crater on Hekla*

Sheets of lava

Sheets of basalt lava cover large areas of Iceland. The largest flowed from a 25 km long fissure in 1783 and covers 565 km². These lava flows give areas of flat plains. Vegetation and fertile soil now cover the older areas.

Waterfalls are common as rivers spill over the edges of hard basalt layers (Figure 6). Rivers have not had enough time to make a more rounded landscape. Hexagonal shaped basalt blocks are made as lava cools slowly.

Figure 6 *Waterfall over basalt*

Figure 7 *Hot water springs*

Figure 8 *A fumarole*

On the boil

Small mud and sulphur cones **and fumaroles** form where hot gases come to the surface (Figure 7). The water is heated below ground when it comes in contact with volcanic rock.

There are hot water springs and **geysers** over most of Iceland (Figure 8). Water reaches the surface at about 75°C though some is at boiling point. Geysers shoot fountains of boiling water 60 m into the air.

Central heating

Boiling water from below ground is used to provide central heating in Iceland's homes. Icelanders claim that their capital, Reykjavik, is the cleanest city in Europe as there is no smoke from burning oil or coal. Natural steam is also used to turn turbines to make electricity.

Exercises

7 What is a sheet lava flow?

8 Draw a sketch of Figure 6. Label in these things:
   waterfall
   basalt rock
   hexagonal shaped rocks in pillars
   broken rock blocks

9 a What does Figure 7 tell you about water in volcanic areas?
   b Explain what is happening in Figure 8.

10 Draw a diagram with labels to show what causes a geyser to erupt.

Northern Ireland's fiery past

In Tertiary times about 30 million years ago, Northern Ireland was part of this spreading ridge as plates pulled apart. Volcanoes erupted and lava flowed over the landscape (Figure 9).

Sometimes only a volcanic **plug** remains to show where the cone used to be (Figure 10). The Antrim Plateau was formed from sheets of basalt.

Forcing through

Layers of molten rock forced their way up through rocks on top. These are called **sills** and **dykes** (Figure 11). They appear on the surface where younger rocks above have been worn down.

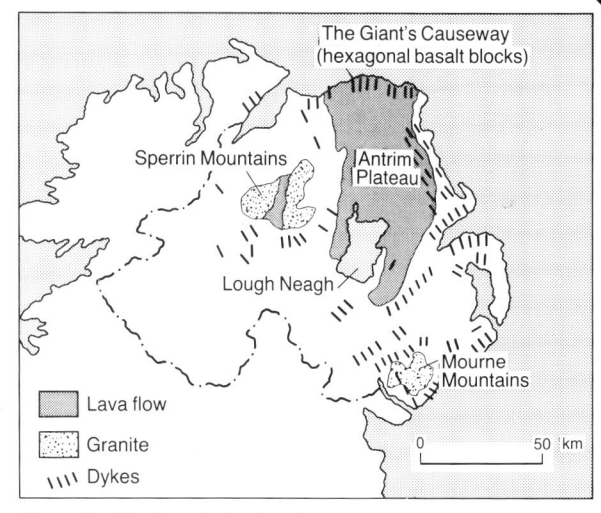

Figure 9 *Northern Ireland geology*

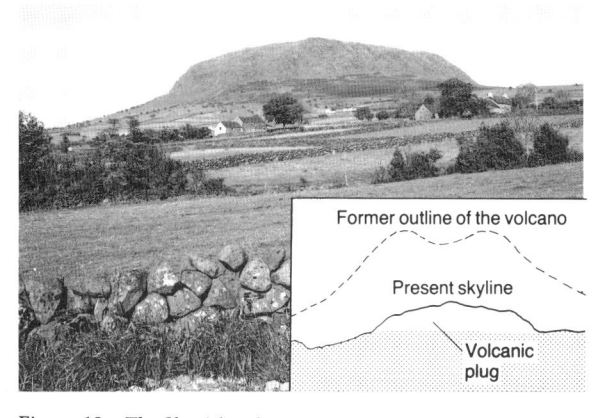

Figure 10 *The Slemish volcanic plug*

Granite mountains

Some molten **magma** did not reach the surface. It welled up into the crust then cooled down to form a granite **batholith**. Erosion has removed the top layers and left the granite as mountains. This is how the Mourne Mountains were formed. Iceland may look like Northern Ireland after the next 30 million years of erosion.

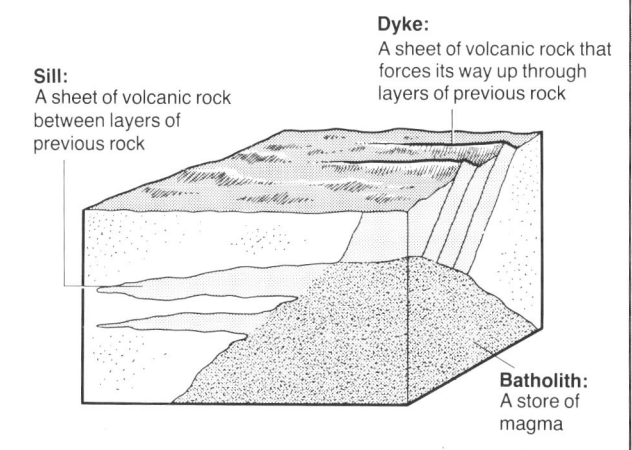

Figure 11 *Igneous intrusions*

Sill: A sheet of volcanic rock between layers of previous rock

Dyke: A sheet of volcanic rock that forces its way up through layers of previous rock

Batholith: A store of magma

Exercises

11 Describe and illustrate the different kinds of evidence which shows that Northern Ireland was once part of a spreading ridge. Mention:
the rocks
the volcanic features
remains of volcanic features

12 a How would you identify a volcanic sill?
b How would you identify a volcanic dyke?
c Explain why Iceland may look like Northern Ireland in the future.

13 List the features of volcanic areas in both Northern Ireland and Iceland that might be of interest to tourists. Explain your list.

6.3 A world of peaks and caverns

A line of limestone peaks runs through the Gunong Mulu National Park in Sarawak (Figure 1). Tropical rain forest partly conceals a world of gorges, caves, cliffs and disappearing streams.

Disappearing streams

Limestone is a rock with distinctive scenery. It is crossed by joints and bedding planes. These make the rock very **permeable**. These natural cracks allow water to pass easily through it. Rain and sometimes streams pass underground.

In Gunong Mulu, surface streams flow over impermeable sandstones until they reach limestone rock (Figure 2). They then disappear down **sinks** which are also called **swallow holes** (Figure 3). These are vertical passages which the streams have carved out of joints.

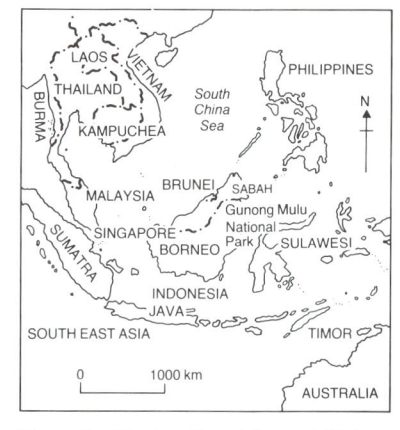

Figure 1   *The location of Gunong Mulu National Park*

Figure 2   *Drainage in Gunong Mulu National Park*

Erosion by solution

The streams erode the limestone with the pebbles and other load they carry. Unlike most rocks, limestone is also attacked by **corrosion**. Rain and stream water are enriched by carbon dioxide from the soil and air. The water acts as a weak carbonic acid which dissolves the limestone.

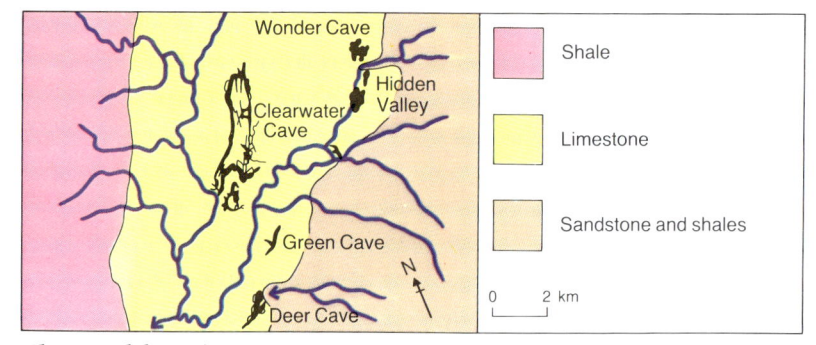

The world underground

Underground streams carve out passages along the joints and bedding planes (Figure 4). The cracks help shape the passages and also result in a complicated cave system (Figure 5). As streams cut lower, caves and tunnels become dry.

Figure 3   *Hidden Valley sink: tracing the stream's course with dye*

Figure 4   *Clearwater River passage*

114

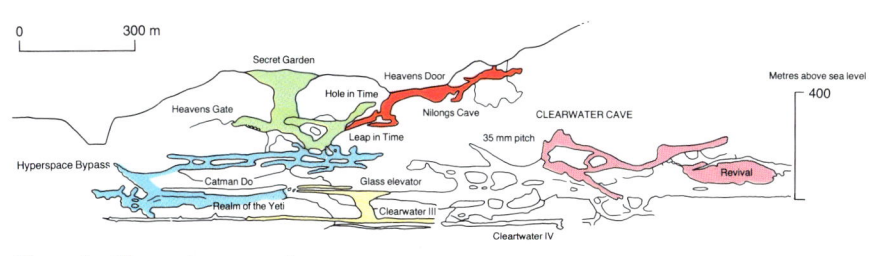

Figure 5 *Clearwater cave system*

Length and depth underground of some Mulu caves

Cave	Length	Depth
Deer Cave	2160 m	over 220 m
Clearwater Cave	51 600 m	355 m
Drunken Forest	1300 m	15 m
Wonder Cave	4770 m	104 m
Cobweb	15 185 m	116 m

Figure 6 *Mulu cavern sizes*

Huge caverns

The limestone can be so riddled with tunnels that their floors and ceilings collapse to form caverns. In Gunong Mulu these are enormous (Figure 6). The Sarawak Chamber is many times bigger than Wembley Stadium.

Interior decoration

Limestone caves often have **stalactites** hanging from their ceilings or **stalagmites** on the floor. The Drunken Forest in Mulu is an example (Figure 7). They form when water drips down from cave roofs and evaporates. The mineral of limestone called **calcite** is deposited.

Rapid solution

The caves and passages are huge for several reasons. They have been forming for up to three million years. Solution erosion is particularly rapid in Sarawak. The annual rainfall of 5700 mm is very high. The dense vegetation and nearby sandstone rocks make the water more acidic and solution more potent.

Figure 7 *Drunken Forest*

Exercises

1 In which country is the Mulu National Park (Figure 1)?

2 a Describe what happens to some streams when they pass over limestone in Gunong Mulu (Figure 2).
   b Make a trace or copy of Figure 2.

3 a What is a sink?
   b How do you think the sink in Figure 3 was made? Mention 'corrosion', 'river load' and 'joints' in your answer.

4 a Use sketches and statistics to show that caves and passages in Gunong Mulu are huge.
   b Give three reasons why they are so large.

Karst scenery

The scenery made by limestone is called **karst**. Features such as disappearing streams and caves are common in all mountain limestone areas. Other features need certain conditions.

For example, the jagged pinnacles of the Mulu Hills form **cone karst**. It has taken several million years for the limestone around them to be worn away. Heavy rain and river erosion were needed and great thicknesses of limestone. Such tower karst covers large areas in the tropics. In south west China it covers 5.2 million km^2 (Figure 8)!

Figure 8   *Cone karst in China*

Figure 9   *Limestone pavement*

Figure 10   *Limestone scars*

Limestone under ice

Limestone pavements were formed under very different conditions. They are found in glaciated areas. The glaciers stripped off layers of limestone along the bedding planes. Since the Ice Age the bare rock of the pavements has been attacked by solution weathering (Figure 9). The rain has picked out and enlarged joints into **grikes**. The grikes separate blocks of limestone called **clints**.

On upper valley sides and often near the pavements are **scars**. The ice and frost shattering broke off blocks of rock along the joints. The cliff-like scars may run for several kilometres. Below them are scree slopes (Figure 10).

Figure 11   *Winnat's Gorge*

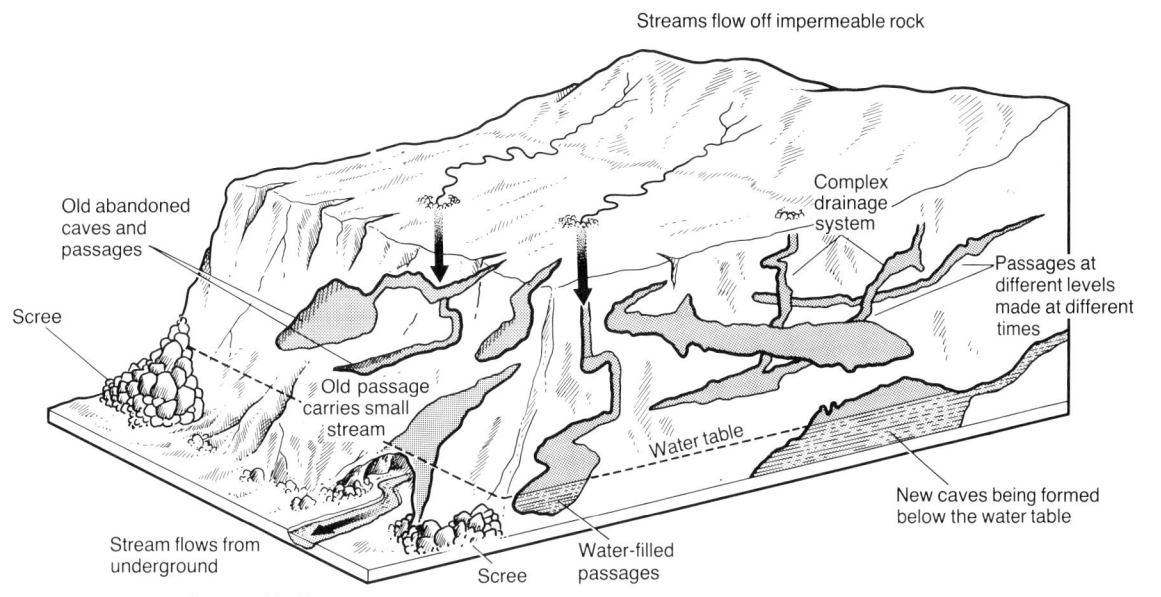

Figure 12 *Water underground in limestone*

Valleys without water

Dry valleys are a common feature of all karst landscapes. Like limestone pavements they are a relic of past conditions. Some, such as Winnat's Gorge in the Peak District, may be collapsed caverns (Figure 11).

Other dry valleys have formed because the water table has fallen. Streams and rain run-off pass through the jointed limestone to reach it (Figure 12).

Figure 13 *A karst landscape*

Exercises

5 a What is karst?
    b Study Figure 13. Make a list of the evidence which shows it is a karst area.
    c Describe how the cone karst in Figure 8 formed.

6 In what way did glaciers alter limestone scenery?

7 a Make a labelled sketch of Figure 11.
    b Name two ways it could have been made.

6.4 Chalk landscapes

Chalk is one of the most easily recognized rocks. Large areas of England are underlain by chalk (Figure 1).

A soft limestone

Chalk is a soft limestone. It is not well-jointed. Instead it is split by many small irregular cracks and some larger 'pipes' (Figure 2). Most rain passes underground and there are few surface streams. The chalk is not strong or jointed enough to have many caves, sinks or karren. The pressure of the overlying rock tends to close up underground cracks.

Chalk uplands

The chalk stands out as higher land. This is the result of the erosion of the softer surrounding rocks and also through folding by earth movements. The chalk is often in the form of a scarp and dip slope (Figure 3).

The chalk uplands are not high. The highest points are just under 300 m. The uplands have names such as **wolds** or **downs**.

Shaped by people

Oak-hazel forest covered the chalk in prehistoric times. Soils were up to a metre thick. When the forests were cleared for farming, fuel and buildings, the soil was eroded. In southern England this was begun by prehistoric people (Figure 4).

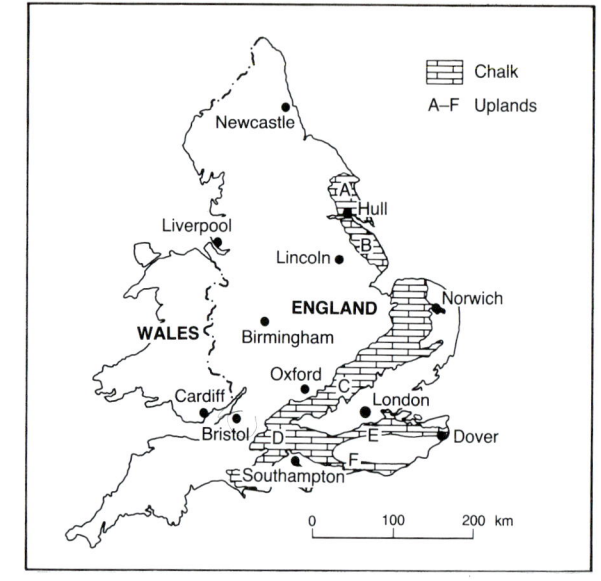

Figure 1 *Chalk areas in England*

Figure 2 *Chalk in close-up*

Figure 3 *A chalk escarpment*

Figure 4 *Chalk landscapes over the centuries*

Figure 5 *Marlborough Downs*

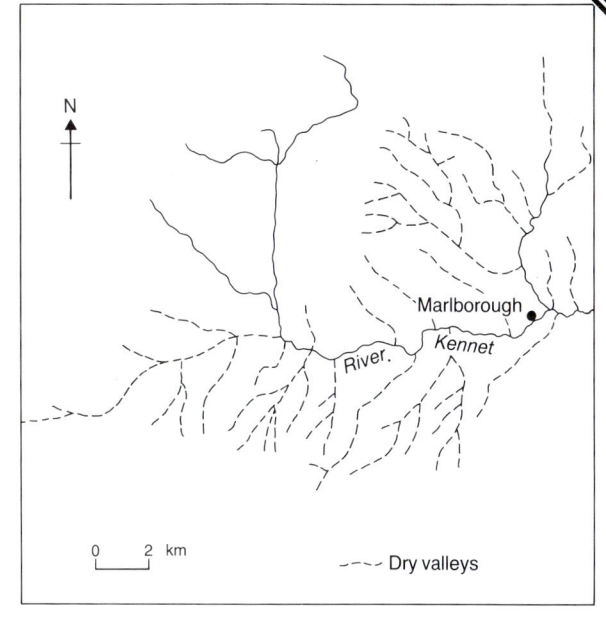

Figure 6 *Dry valleys in the Marlborough Downs*

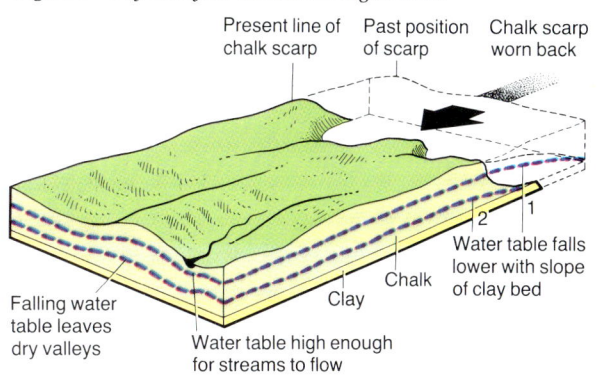

Figure 7 *How some dry valleys are formed*

Open and rolling

Today the soil is thin. The underlying chalk shows through ploughed land and paths. Once removed, it is difficult for woods to grow again. Chalk country has an open rolling appearance (Figure 5). Because there are few streams and rain sinks underground, chalk areas are less carved up than other rocks.

Dry valleys

Dry valleys are widespread (Figure 6). As with other limestone rocks, some were carved several thousand years ago when the rainfall and water table were higher. Others, on scarp slopes, were formed in cold periods during the Ice Age when the ground was frozen. **Solifluction** moved the soil and weathered rock downhill. It is thought that many dip slope valleys became dry because the nearby chalk escarpment was eroded back (Figure 7).

Exercises

1. Name the chalk uplands marked on Figure 1.

2. In what ways is chalk different from some other limestones?

3. Use Figures 4 and 7 to explain how the Marlborough Downs landscape in Figure 5 could have developed.

6.5 Landscapes of technology

It is said that 'faith can move mountains'. Nowadays, explosives, excavators and power shovels can do the same job.

Early earthmovers

Changing the landscape is nothing new. In Britain, the **artificial** Silbury Hill was built about 3000 years ago, perhaps as a grave. The work was done using antler picks and bone shovels (Figure 1).

In Asia, terraces cut into steep hillsides are a traditional way of making space and holding back water for growing rice (Figure 2). Human labour is still needed to do the work.

Figure 1 *Silbury Hill in Wiltshire*

Figure 2 *Terraced slopes in Indonesia*

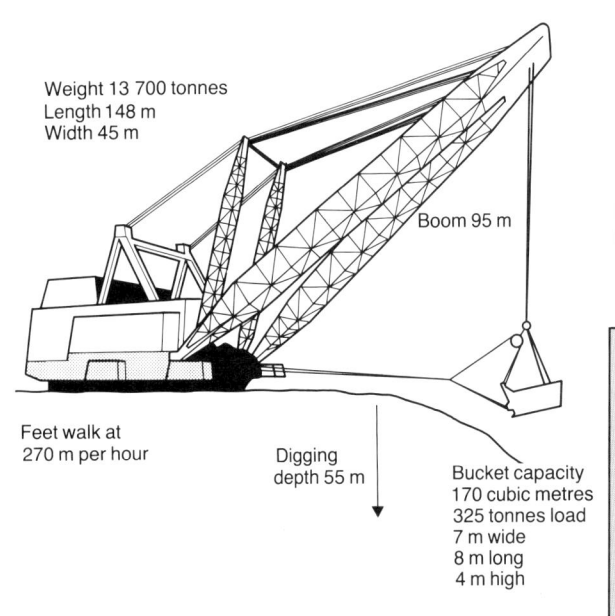

Weight 13 700 tonnes
Length 148 m
Width 45 m
Boom 95 m
Feet walk at 270 m per hour
Digging depth 55 m
Bucket capacity
170 cubic metres
325 tonnes load
7 m wide
8 m long
4 m high

Figure 3 *The Big Muskie*

Changing gear

More powerful **technology** is now able to change the landscape on an increasing scale. The 'Big Muskie' **dragline** has a bucket which scoops out 225 tonnes of earth at a time (Figure 3). Machines such as this can create a whole new landscape.

Exercises

1. What does Silbury Hill tell you about the people who built it? (Hint: skills, equipment, organization, time, beliefs.)

2. Describe the scene in Figure 2. Include:
   where it is
   how the slopes have been changed
   why the terraces have been needed

3. a Give some examples of the kind of jobs where large earthmoving equipment needs to be used.
   b Use the dragline figures to explain why this kind of technology is used.

Digging deep

The largest artificial holes are caused by **opencast** mining where the mineral is near the surface. The opencast copper mine in Utah, USA is the world's largest (Figure 4). It is 3.7 km across, 774 m deep and covers 7.3 km². Mining began in 1904. Since then, almost 5 000 000 000 tonnes of rock have been removed!

Figure 4   *Bingham Copper Mine in Utah*

Piling high

Opencast mining usually leaves vast amounts of waste rock. At Bingham, 2300 tonnes of waste rock has to be removed to get 1 tonne of copper ore. In every tonne of ore, there is only 6.5 kg of copper.

In the past, waste rock from mining was piled into cone-shaped tips (Figure 5). Today, waste is landscaped into flatter shapes or used to fill in old quarries. Grasses are sown to make the landscape look attractive again.

Figure 5   *China clay waste tip in Cornwall*

Sinking ground

Underground mining and water extraction causes **subsidence**. This damages buildings and can cause flooding in lowlying areas. The North Sea bed is said to be sinking because of oil extraction. Water extraction is partly to blame for making Venice sink into the sea.

Exercises

4   a What has been mined at Bingham?
    b Why are the workings at Bingham called opencast?
    c Describe the unusual shape of the mine.

5   a Why does mining involve so much waste rock?
    b What problems can be caused when waste rock is removed? Think about:
       unsightliness
       danger of collapse
    c How can tips of waste rock be made more attractive or put to use? Give some ideas. Draw and label some sketches to illustrate your ideas.

6   Do you have any ideas which would:
    a slow down the speed of mining subsidence
    b stop subsidence in areas where there is oil or water extraction?

Changing water to land

The Netherlands is a small but densely populated country. It is hard to find enough space for everybody's needs. This is one reason why Dutch engineers have become expert at making dry land from lakes and the sea bed (Figure 6).

Reclamation schemes

Two modern **reclamation** schemes are in Lake Ijssel and the Rhine delta. Large areas of Lake Ijssel have been enclosed by dykes and pumped dry to make **polders** (Figure 7). The polders must be kept dry by pumps. They are about 5 m below sea level and water cannot drain away naturally.

In the delta area, dams protect lowlying islands from being flooded. Mud flats and marshland have also been reclaimed to give more space for the port of Europoort (Figure 8).

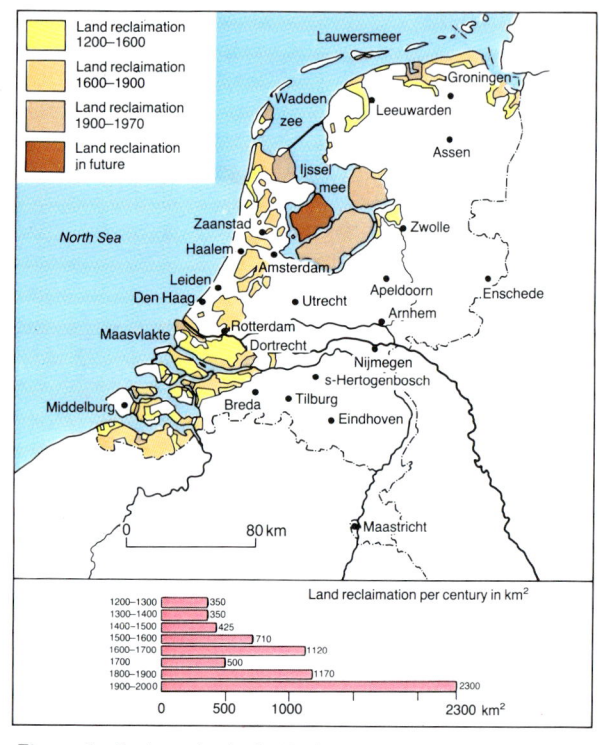

Figure 6 *Reclamation in the Netherlands*

Figure 7 *New polder farmland*

Figure 8 *Reclaimed land at Europoort*

Exercise

7   a Explain the term reclamation.
    b What is a polder?
    c Why does water have to be pumped out of polders?
    d Why do the Dutch people go to so much expense and trouble, making polders?
       Think about:
       flood control, river and sea
       population density
       space for different types of land use

Land to water

New food and water supplies are needed by the increasing world population. **Reservoirs** are needed to provide the extra water.

In Egypt, the Aswan High Dam can hold back 164 000 million m³ of water in Lake Nasser (Figures 9, 11). This gives a regular supply of water to farms in an area that is desert.

The water also provides power for a hydro-electric power station (Figure 10). The lake is planned to give fish supplies of up to 80 000 tonnes each year.

Silting up

New lakes, such as at Aswan, can cause problems. Over 100 million tonnes of silt comes down the River Nile each year. Some of this is now trapped behind the dam. One guess is that about 30 000 million m³ of silt will have settled in the lake in 500 years time. The silt no longer reaches the Nile Delta where it used to make new land. This will make the delta easier to erode by the sea.

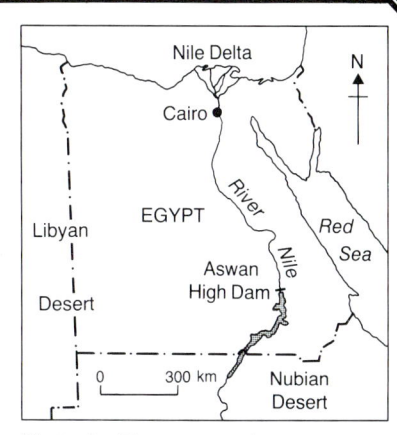

Figure 9 *The Aswan High Dam in Egypt*

Figure 10 *Power from the Aswan High Dam*

Figure 11 *Lake Nasser*

Exercises

8   a Why are reservoirs needed?
    b Give details of the Aswan High Dam to show how it has changed the landscape.
    c What dangers can be caused by building dams and creating reservoirs?
    d Why do some reservoirs have a limited life?

9   Why is people's effect on the landscape going to increase even more in the future?

Side effects

The Aswan High Dam is near an area of active faulting. One fear is that the extra weight of water might trigger off an earthquake. Damage to the dam would cause enormous flooding in densely populated towns and rural areas.

New methods in new places

One thing is certain. Places which were once too remote or inhospitable, are no longer safe from change. As resources are used up and prices rise, it becomes worthwhile building the technology to overcome the problems.

Glossary

Abrasion: wearing away by a rubbing action /3.2, 3.4, 4.2
Abstraction: taking water out of a river /3.3
Acid lava: a lava rich in silica which flows slowly /6.2
Active: (volcano) still likely to erupt /6.2
Active layer: surface of permafrost which thaws in summer /4.4
Aeolian sand: wind-blown sand /5.5
Afforestation: planting trees on a large scale /3.3
Agents of erosion: different ways by which land is worn away /3.1
Alluvium: soil made from material carried in rivers /3.2
Alveoloes: honeycombed rocks in arid areas /2.2
Angle of repose: angle at which loose debris rests /2.3
Anticline: the top part of a folded structure /1.4
Aquifer: rock strata which stores water /5.4
Arches: cliffs tunnelled through by the sea /3.4
Area: (river) the cross-section measurement /3.2
Arêtes: narrow ridges shaped by corrie glaciers /4.2
Arid: very dry area or climate /5.1
Artificial: made by people and not nature /6.5
Atmosphere: the layer of gases which surround the earth /1.2
Attrition: rock broken up by grinding together /3.2, 3.4

Backwash: water flowing back down a beach /3.4
Bar: a bank of material built up by waves /3.4
Barchan: crescent-shaped dune /5.5
Badlands: landscape scarred by gulleying /5.3
Basic lava: lava with little silica which flows quickly /6.2
Basins: large depressions in the land /1.4
Batholith: a dome-shaped mass of igneous rock which cooled under the surface /6.2
Bays: curved inlets in the coast /3.4
Bedding plane: the surface between layers of sedimentary rock /1.2
Biosphere: places which support the Earth's plants and animals /1.2
Block faulting: plateaus and basins formed between fault lines /1.4
Breaker: a wave where the water particles break their circular motion and the crest falls forward /3.4

Calcite: the mineral of limestone /6.3
Caldera: a volcano which has collapsed /1.3
Cambering: widening of joints as rock strata slip downslope /2.3
Catchment area: the area water comes from into a river system /3.2

Channel: the shape in which a river flows /3.2
Chemical weathering: breaking up and altering of rock by the weather /2.2
Climates: different systems of weather /1.2
Clints: the blocks in limestone pavements /6.3
Clitter: boulders on the lower slopes of tors /2.2
Cone karst: a limestone landscape of steep isolated hills /6.3
Constructive: (waves) that build up a beach /3.4
Constructive plate margin: where new crust is being formed as two plates pull apart /1.3
Continental plates: plates which have a continent on them /1.3
Continents: very large land masses /1.3
Contour ploughing: ploughing along the same height on hillslopes /2.4, 3.3
Convection currents: flows caused by rising heat /1.3
Core sample: a sample of rock from a bore-hole /1.5
Corrie glaciers: glaciers flowing from corries /4.2
Corries: large mountain hollows where some glaciers formed /4.2
Corrosion: chemical corrosion such as dissolving away /6.3
Crags: inland rock cliffs /2.3
Crevasses: deep cracks in the surface of glaciers /4.2
Cross-section: a vertical slice downwards /3.2
Crust: the hard top layer of rock around the Earth /1.2
Currents: (sea) flows of water in a particular direction /3.4

Dams: walls built to hold back water /3.3
Delta: river material built up into a fan shape /3.2, 3.4
Dendritic: a pattern of drainage shaped like tree branches /3.2
Denudation: wearing away the landscape by weathering and erosion /6.1
Deposited: laid down /3.4
Deposition: the process of laying down transported materials /3.2
Deposits: materials that have been laid down /1.5
Desalination plants: large works purifying sea water /5.4
Desert crust: desert surface with high salt content /5.3
Desertification: making a desert, usually through the misuse of land /2.4
Destructive: (waves) that remove beach material /3.4
Destructive plate margin: where plates are moving towards each other and being destroyed /1.3
Discharge: the amount of water flowing along a river /3.2
Dissected: cut down into the landscape /3.2

Dormant: (volcano) which has not erupted for a long time /6.2
Downs: chalk uplands /6.4
Dragline: a large machine for removing top layers of earth /6.5
Drainage basin: the area drained by a river system /3.2
Dry valleys: valleys with rivers no longer in them /6.3
Dykes: layers of igneous rock which have forced their way up through overlying strata /3.5
Earthflow: regolith saturated enough to move downslope /2.3
Earthquake belts: areas where earthquakes are most common /1.3
Elbow of capture: the sharp bend where a river has been captured by another river system /3.2
Energy: the ability to perform types of work /3.2, 3.4
Environments: places with a unique landscape /1.2
Erosion: wearing away / 2.2, 3.1
Escarpment: a steep slope along an area of upland /1.4
Eskers: winding ridges left by meltwater streams /4.5
Estuaries: large inlets where rivers flow into the sea /3.4, 3.5
Etching: small shapes carved in rock by wind blast /5.5
Eustatic: changes in land and sea levels due to a rise or fall of the sea /4.5
Exposed: uncovered by erosion /2.2
Extinct: (volcano) which will never erupt again /6.2

Famine: severe lack of food due to crop failure /2.4
Fault: a break through the rock strata /1.4
Fault line: the line along which rock strata has broken /1.4
Fetch: the unbroken stretch of water over which waves travel and build up /3.4
Fiords: glacial valleys drowned by the sea /4.5
Fissure eruption: a volcanic eruption along a line /6.2
Flash floods: sudden floods /5.3
Flood: water that overflows its channel /3.2
Flood plain: the valley bottom land liable to river flooding /3.2
Floodway: a channel dug out to divert flood water /3.3
Fluting: small rock grooves made by wind blast /5.5
Fluvioglacial: made by meltwater streams / 4.5
Folds: bends in rock strata /1.4
Foreland: a triangular shaped piece of coast /3.4
Fossil: the imprint of past plant or animal life /1.4
Fossil fuels: fuels from rocks such as coal, oil, gas /1.5
Friction: rubbing together /3.2
Frost heaving: pushing up of ground by ground ice /4.4
Frost weathering: action of frost in breaking up the surface /2.2

Fumaroles: holes through which volcanic gases escape /6.2

Gabions: wire cages filled with rock to prevent erosion /3.3
Geologists: scientists who study rocks /1.1
Geomorphology: the study of landforms /1.1
Geothermal: heat from deep in the Earth's crust /1.5
Geyser: an eruption of boiling water /1.5, 6.2
Gibber plain (reg): vast desert rock pavement /5.1
Glacial hazard: a danger from ice sheets or glaciers /4.3
Glacial ice: ice made from compressed snow /4.2
Glacials: cold periods during the Ice Age /4.1
Gorge: a deep narrow valley /3.2
Granular disintegration: the breaking up of rock into grains /2.2
Grikes: widened joints in limestone pavements /6.3
Ground water: water found underground /5.4
Growan: coarse sand left by the weathering of granite /2.2
Groynes: barriers built on a beach /3.5
Gullies: deep eroded channels /5.3
Gulls: enlarged joints which result from cambering /2.3
Gully erosion: the carving up of land into deep grooves by running water /2.4

Habitats: environments in which animals live /3.5
Hanging valleys: tributary valleys left high up the sides of a glaciated valley /4.2
Hard pan: hard layer cemented by salts below a desert surface /5.3
Headland: land which juts out into the sea /3.4
Helical air-flow: eddying flow of air forming dunes /5.5
High: (tide) the normal maximum level of the sea along the coast /3.4
High diurnal range: a wide difference between the highest and lowest temperatures in a day /5.2
Hydraulic action: wearing away by the force of flowing water /3.2, 3.4
Hydrograph: a graph to show river discharge and time /3.2
Hydrolysis: the chemical action of water in weathering /2.2
Hydrosphere: the areas of water on the Earth /1.2
Hypothesis: an idea put forward to explain how and why something happens /3.4

Ice Age: cold geological period when ice sheets spread /4.1
Ice avalanche: sudden fall of ice into a valley /4.3

Ice cap: large sheet of ice covering high land /4.2
Ice surge: sudden forward movement of a glacier /4.3
Ice wedge: crack in ground filled and enlarged by ice /4.4
Igneous: (rock) from under the crust /1.2
Impermeable: (rock) which does not allow water to sink through /1.2
Inland drainage: the draining of streams inland /5.3
Inselbergs: isolated hills in tropical and desert areas /2.2
Insolation weathering: the breaking up of rock due to temperature changes /5.2
Integrated Project in Arid Lands (IPAL): Kenyan scheme to improve life of people in arid areas /2.4
Inter-glacials: warmer periods during the Ice Age /4.1
Isostatic: a change in land and sea levels due to the land rising /4.5

Joints: vertical lines of weakness in rock strata /1.2

Karren: solution grooves made by running water /2.2
Karst: a landscape of many limestone landforms /6.3

Lagoons: shallow coastal areas enclosed behind a natural barrier /3.4
Landforms: physical features with characteristic shapes /1.2
Land management: careful, planned use of the land /2.4
Land mass: a large area of land such as a continent /1.3
Landslides: rapid sliding of 'dry' rock downslope /2.3
Landslip: rock which has slipped downslope /2.3
Lateral: sideways /3.2
Lava cone: a cone-shaped mound of lava /6.2
Levees: ridges built up along river banks /3.2
Limestone pavements: weathered, eroded, level surfaces of bare limestone rock /6.3
Lithosphere: the Earth's rock layers /1.2
Longshore drift: material being moved mainly in one direction along a coastline /3.4
Low: (tide) the normal lowest level of the tide along the coast /3.4

Magma: molten material from the Earth's mantle /1.3, 6.2
Meandering: (a river) flowing in a series of large bends /3.2
Mechanical weathering: the breaking up of rock by physical weathering /2.2, 5.2
Meltwater: water from melting ice /4.5
Meltwater streams: streams formed from melting ice /4.2, 4.3

Metamorphic: (rock) a change from one type of rock to another /1.2
Minerals: the separate materials which make rocks /1.2
Moraine: debris carried and left by glaciers /4.2
Mud flats: areas of shallow water along a coast where mud is exposed at low tide /3.4

Neap: (tide) times when there is the lowest difference between high and low tide /3.4
Nomadic pastoralists: herders who move with their animals in search of pasture and water /2.4
Normal fault: a fault where rock pulls apart and one side slides down along another /1.4
No-till cropping: growing crops on land where the remains of the previous crop have not been ploughed in /2.4
Nunataks: peaks sticking through ice sheets /4.2

Oceanic plates: plates with an ocean on top /1.3
Opencast: removing rocks near the surface by quarrying /6.5
Order: to arrange in a list based on size /3.2
Ores: rocks which contain a metal /1.5
Orogeny: a geological time when mountains are built /1.4
Outwash deposits: material left by meltwater streams /4.5
Outwash fans: fan-shaped heaps of debris left by meltwater streams /4.5
Outwash plains: lowlands covered by outwash deposits /4.5
Overflow channel: a channel cut by a stream overflowing from an ice-dammed lake /4.5
Overgrazed: removal of vegetation by too much grazing /2.4
Ox-bow: (lake) left after a meander changes course /3.2

Parallel retreat of slopes: wearing back of slopes at a constant angle /2.3
Patterned ground: stone strips and polygons shaped by frost heaving /4.4
Pediments: tropical or desert plains carved in solid rock /5.3
Percolation: sinking of water underground /5.3
Periglacial: areas on the fringes of ice sheets /4.4
Permafrost: deeply frozen ground /4.4
Permeable: (rock) which allows water to sink through /1.2
Pillow lava: a rounded lava formed on the ocean bed /1.3
Pingoes: hills caused by frost heaving /4.4

Planets: very large masses of rock in orbit around a star /1.2
Plateaus: steep-sided upland areas with level tops /1.4
Plate margin: the boundary between two plates /1.3
Plates: large separate slabs of crust /1.3
Plucking: see **quarrying** /4.2
Plug: solidified lava in the neck of a volcano /6.2
Pluvial period: Past time with a higher rainfall /5.3
Polders: areas of land reclaimed from lakes or the sea /6.5
Pools: deeper sections along the course of a river /3.2
Pressure release: jointing caused by removal of the weight of overlying rocks /2.2
Pyramidal peak: jagged mountain top shaped by frost and ice action /4.2

Quarrying (plucking): erosion by ice tearing out rock to which it is frozen /3.4, 4.2

Radial: (drainage) a pattern of rivers that flow out in all directions from a central area /3.2
Raised beaches: beaches moved above the level of the waves /4.5
Reclaim: to win back and put land to a new use /3.5
Reclamation: changing land to a new, improved use /6.5
Reg: see **gibber plains** /5.1
Regime: the annual flow pattern of a river /3.2
Regolith: surface layer of soil and weathered material /2.1
Relief: the shape of the land /1.2
Reservoirs: lakes made by building a dam /6.5
Resistant: hard to wear away /1.2, 3.4
Reverse fault: a fault line when rock moves together and one side slides over the other /1.4
Revetments: walls built along a river's channel sides /3.3
Rias: deep inlets formed when sea level rose /4.5
Richter scale: a scale of measurement for earthquakes /1.5
Ridge: a long narrow piece of high land /1.3
Riffles: shallow stretches of water in a river /3.2
Rift valley: a valley with fault escarpments on both sides /1.4
Rill erosion: removal of soil by small streams of water /2.4
River capture: when the water from one stream system is diverted into another /3.2
River system: the network of streams and rivers in a drainage basin /3.2
Roche moutonée: rock smoothed and plucked by ice /4.2

Rock basin lakes: lakes in hollows scoured out by ice /4.2
Rock cycle: the way in which rocks change from one type to another over long periods of time /1.2
Rocks: solid earth material /1.2
Row crops: crops planted in rows /2.4
Run-off: water that flows down slopes into a river system /3.2

Salination: salts entering the soil and making it infertile /2.4
Saltation: wind moving the sand in a jumping action /5.5
Salt weathering: the breaking up of rock by salts /5.2
Sandblasting: erosion by wind-blown sand /5.5
Sand dunes: hills of sand /3.4
Sayf: long winding sand ridge running parallel to the wind /5.5
Scars: long limestone crags /6.3
Screes: weathered rock at the foot of slopes /2.2
Sea floor spreading: the process of new rock being formed on the ocean bed as plates pull apart /1.3
Seams: bands of a rock such as coal /1.5
Seaside resorts: coastal towns with tourist facilities /3.5
Sedimentary: (rock) formed from pieces of plants, animals or other rocks /1.2
Seismic survey: a method of mapping geological structures by using sound waves /1.5
Semi-arid: a dry climate, almost a desert /2.4
Sheet erosion: removal of soil by sheet flow /2.4
Sheet flow: flow of water over the ground as a thin sheet /2.3
Shield: (volcano) with very shallow-angled slopes /6.2
Shingle: a mass of rounded stones usually forming a beach /3.4
Silt: fine muds carried downstream in a river /3.2
Sinks: vertical openings in limestone down which streams disappear /6.3
Slope decline: wearing down of slope to a more gentle angle /2.3
Slump: where a cliff becomes unstable and collapses /3.5
Snowfield: large area in mountains where snow builds up /4.2
Soil: the top layer of the regolith containing plant food /2.4
Soil conservation: protecting soil from erosion /2.4
Soil creep: movement of soil downslope under gravity /2.3
Soil erosion: removal of soil by wind or running water /2.4

Solar system: a group of planets around a sun /1.2
Solifluction: the movement of thawed weathered rock downhill /6.4
Solution: a process of wearing away by dissolving /2.2, 3.2
Solution weathering: weathering rock by dissolving it /2.2
Spit: a sand or shingle bank which grows out to sea /3.4
Spring: (tide) the times when the tidal difference is greatest /3.4
Springs: places where water comes out of rock /3.2
Stabilized: not likely to move /3.4
Stack: a piece of rock left surrounded by the sea as the coast wears back /3.4
Stalactites: calcite deposits hanging from the ceilings of limestone passages and caves /6.3
Stalagmites: stacks of calcite on the floors of limestone caves and passages /6.3
Storage: water held back in the rocks /3.2
Storm ridge: a ridge of stones on a beach which marks where the highest waves have reached /3.4
Strata: a layer of one type of rock /1.4
Striations: scratches on rock made by moving ice /4.2
Strip cropping: growing crops across slopes to prevent soil erosion /2.4
Structure: the way in which strata is lying /1.4
Subsidence: when the ground sinks /6.5
Surface wash: washing away of regolith by raindrop impact or sheet flow /2.3
Suspension: the process of carrying material along in wind or water /5.5
Swales: wide 'hollows' between sand ridges /5.5
Swallow holes: see 'sinks' /6.3
Swash: waves moving up a beach /3.4
Syncline: the bottom part of a folded structure /1.4
System: a unit made up of linked parts /1.2

Tear fault: a break in rock strata as one side slips sideways /1.4
Technology: the use of science and machinery /6.5
Tidal range: the height difference between high and low tide /3.4
Tidal scour: the action of tides removing material /3.4
Tombola: a spit which joins the mainland to an island /3.4
Top soil: surface layer of soil containing most plant food /2.4
Tors: rocky hilltops exposed by weathering /2.2
Transportation: movement /3.2
Transverse dunes: dunes extending across the path of the wind /5.5
Trellis: a river drainage pattern with tributary streams flowing at right angles to the main river /3.2
Trenches: long narrow deep parts of the ocean bed /1.3
Tropical weathering: breaking up of rock by tropical climates /2.2
Truncated spurs: the cut-back and straightened sides of a glaciated valley /4.2

U-shaped troughs: deep valleys carved by glaciers /4.2
Utilidors: insulated boxes carrying service pipes in cold climates /4.4

Valley glaciers: ice flowing down valleys /4.2
Velocity: speed /3.2
Vertical erosion: wearing downwards /3.2
Volcanic cone: a volcano in a cone shape /1.3

Wadis: dry desert valleys /5.3
Water Authorities: organizations responsible for water control and supplies /3.3
Water budget: the amount of water in a system /3.2
Water cycle: the way in which water changes from one form to another from sea to land and back again /3.2
Watershed: the higher land between two drainage basins /3.2
Water table: the level below which rock is saturated with water /3.2
Water transfer: taking water from one place to somewhere else /3.3
Water vapour: water as a gas /3.2
Wave-cut platform: the flat rock area left as a coast wears back /3.4
Wave refraction: the change of direction of waves as they approach a shore /3.4
Waves: the uneven surface of the sea caused by wind /3.4
Weather: the day-to-day climatic conditions /1.2
Weathering: breaking up the Earth's surface by the action of the weather /2.1, 3.2
Wetted perimeter: the sides and bed of a river in contact with flowing water /3.2
Wind blast: erosion by the force of the wind /5.5
Wind deflation: creation of hollows due to the removal of sand by the wind /5.5
Wind gap: a dry valley in a range of hills which may have been caused by river capture, once thought to be caused by wind erosion /3.2
Wolds: chalk uplands /6.4

Yardangs: rocks smoothed and rounded by wind erosion /5.5